"I've been coming to thes[...]
and this is the first time I'[...]
room totally riveted for nearly an hour and a half.
Shelley is absolutely brilliant!"

A.F. Sainsburys Supermarkets

"The feedback from the delegates was the best we've
ever had. Thank you for a brilliant presentation"

D.G. BT Openreach

To find out more about how to
book Shelley as a speaker for
your event, please visit:
www.stand-upforyourself.com

Alternatively, please contact
Shelley direct at:
shelley@stand-upforyourself.com

IN PRAISE OF
STAND-UP FOR YOURSELF

There are writers who merely write words and then there are writers who craft emotional moments in our lives.

If the happenings of an ever increasingly plundered world turns your face away
And saddens your shoulders…

Stop!

Take time right now — to join a true traveler of time in her journey of unearthing the truth — both for herself and those she encountered along the path.

I cried and wept.

I laughed and chortled.

I sat and thought and changed.

You will too.

Time will confirm it was for the better.

Peter Thomson
"The UK's Most Prolific Information Product Creator"

Anyone performing Stand-Up deserves respect. To do it after overcoming life threatening illness and overcoming the obstacles in this story is truly remarkable. If you need uplifting, read this story.

Caroline Lucas, MP
Former Leader of The Green Party

Brilliant, captivating and thought-provoking. Shelley shares her story with such honesty and openness. Highly recommended.

Peggy McColl
New York Times Best-Selling Author

If you buy one inspirational book this year make it this one.

Jo Good
BBC radio presenter

Shelley Bridgman is unique, her book and her life is full of humour and honesty, she is a stunning writer and brings to life her amazing true story. Don't miss this.

Janey Godley
Best-Selling Author & Top Scottish Comic

Shelley Bridgman is an inspirational woman. A truly moving and wonderful piece of story-telling that must be read by everyone. This is a biography, a self-help book, and a wonderfully entertaining read — all in one book.

Shazia Mirza
Award-Winning Comedian

Shelley Bridgman is a woman with not just one perspective on life, but many. A born traveler, her journey has taken her not only around the world, but around herself, observing her own life from every angle, even as the smooth exterior began to crack. It is only after entering through those cracks that this extraordinary and brave woman was able to work from the inside to create a strong, shimmering self, that is entirely her own. Told with intelligence, honesty and humility, hers is a story unlike any other, and yet it speaks to all of us.

Paul Lucas
New York Producer

Shelley's story is uplifting and heart-warming, and shows her strength and courage as she lives each day with humour in whatever comes her way.

Emma Ziff
Broadcaster & Writer

I love this book — the laugh out loud funny moments amongst the smiles, my own trips down Memory Lane as I lived with Shelley through her story, the vivid retelling of London through those Swinging Sixties years, the anecdotes about the 60s groups (as we then called them) like the Stones and the Who, the sense of reliving through past decades now gone forever, the achingly honest account of her journey, the insights she gained and the reflections she stirred in me. I knew some of Shelley's story as she is now a dear friend and subject of a chapter in *The Inspiring Journeys of Pilgrim Mothers* but this wonderful book added such fabulous, rich detail to her life. Shelley is for me a true Pilgrim Mother, a female pioneer, courageous, at the forefront of change and leading the way whilst caring for and keeping together her family with the support of her partner. This is by turns a love story, a memoir, a comedy, a tragedy and lots more. I was engaged, encouraged and entertained by her story. Read it and discover more about Shelley's fascinating story for yourself.

Jane Noble Knight
Best-selling Author, Speaker and Mentor

STAND-UP FOR YOURSELF

STAND-UP FOR YOURSELF

…And become the hero or shero you were born to be

SHELLEY BRIDGMAN
STAND-UP PUBLISHING

Stand-Up for YourSelf: And become the hero or shero you were born to be

Copyright © 2014 Shelley Bridgman

www.stand-upforyourself.com

Editors: Christine Messier (www.YourVoiceInc.com)

Naomi Fowler (www.naomifowler.org)

Copyeditor: Jane Noble Knight (www.thepilgrimmother.com)

Proofreader: Valerie Hardware

Design and typesetting: Tanya Bäck (www.tanyabackdesigns.com)

Cover art and cover design: Jane Dixon-Smith (www.jdsmith-design.com)

Cover concept: Carole Railton (www.livingsuccess.co.uk)

Photography: Ingrid Mårn Global Diversity Photography

Hair: Bryn at Easton Regal (www.eastonregal.com)

Printer: Lightning Source

First published 2014 in the United Kingdom by Stand-up Publishing

www.stand-uppublishing.com

ISBN: 978-0-9575712-0-4

TO MARIE
For the gift of unconditional love

CONTENTS

INTRODUCTION

For much of my life I have tried to hide from the world to avoid being seen. When I was young, I feared rejection by the children at school. As an adult I feared losing my business and everything I had worked for. As a parent I feared for my children, feared that because of me they would be bullied or victimised. When I began this writing project, the same fears rose up inside me. What will people think of me? Will I be rejected? Will people condemn me?

Then I realised my bigger fear was to *give way* to those fears and to silence myself when others like me around the world are prevented from having that voice.

So why write a book documenting my life with all the warts, all the highs and all the lows and why now?

For one, I always feel a sense of incredulity when a twenty-five-year-old tells his or her life story. No matter what amazing achievements they may have had, how can they have lived a full life? On the other hand, some twenty-five-year-olds may have lived fuller lives than many octogenarians … so perhaps I simply wasn't ready.

I trust the reader will enjoy my journey from birth and earliest memories through adolescence and confusion via great lows and darkest moments, followed by life-changing experiences and the highs of travelling to exotic lands and eventually finding myself. As a child growing up on a council estate in West London I had no idea that one day I would look back on such polarities of joy and sorrow, such a roller-coaster of emotions and experiences.

I have documented my change of gender which, although a dramatic sounding act, is in itself actually very simple. It was the fear and then the reality of much of the world's reaction that caused the worry and the stress. Perhaps it was the struggle for me to accept myself which presented the greatest challenge.

My grandmother gifted me a love for travel and as with life I have enjoyed the journey as much as the destination. My childhood journey took me to church every Sunday where I listened to one boring speaker after another, trying to convince me that God loved me or that Jesus wanted me 'for a sunbeam'. It was a message that sounded hollow and seemed without foundation. I didn't believe he existed and I certainly didn't believe he loved me. Where was the evidence?

In my teens, I looked into other religions: Islam, Buddhism, Hinduism, Sufism and just about anything anyone had written about and called religion. I wanted to believe in an afterlife but I couldn't find the answer. Reading Kahlil Gibran, a visit to a medium, and my experience on Lake Titicaca were all pointers on my journey. Not for me the 'Paul on the Road to Damascus' experience but a gradual realisation that I was more than the body I walked around in.

Although my life has in many respects been dominated by the conflict with my gender identity, I trust the reader will feel my life has been much more. I hope that by sharing my journey with you, you will find elements that might at best inspire you but anyway will help you hold up a mirror of understanding to your own life and your own unique experiences.

More than anything, I trust you will enjoy reading my story.

Shelley Bridgman

PROLOGUE

Life is sometimes cruel. Life is sometimes terribly, *terribly* cruel. I am standing in what was once called Palestine at the grave of my little sister who I never met. My heart is aching but my tears aren't just *my* tears. They are tears for my teenage mother who never even saw this final resting place ... never had closure. They are tears for my sister who only knew life for four months but somehow lived on through me. Tears for the pain I've carried all my life from both of them.

Fifty years later I have finally found her resting place. I am standing here for all our sakes. I feel strangely peaceful.

With a muffled honk of his car horn my Israeli taxi driver breaks the early morning silence and brings me back to 1990. A glance at my watch tells me I need to return to my duties running the convention an hour away in Tel Aviv.

The cool morning air dries the hot tears on my cheeks. The pre-dawn grey of the cemetery is now bathed in sunshine. It looks surprisingly green and fresh.

I blow my sister a kiss and I walk back to my impatient driver.

1
CREATION AND BEGINNINGS

SORRY BUT THIS MIGHT HURT A BIT!

*"A thing constructed can only be loved after it is constructed;
but a thing created is loved before it exists."*
Charles Dickens

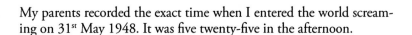

My parents recorded the exact time when I entered the world screaming on 31st May 1948. It was five twenty-five in the afternoon.

Even at the moment of birth I wanted to express myself. Perhaps I already felt I had something to say. But I soon learned that expressing myself, being who I am and feeling good about it was going to be a long struggle. It would take me on a very painful life journey, causing a lot of suffering to myself and those close to me before I experienced the joy of self-realisation and fulfilment.

I was diagnosed male and given the name of Michael. I was a 'baby-boomer', born in a prefab (temporary housing which was common in post-war Britain) home on a council estate in Northolt, West London. Looking back, perhaps everything was temporary in my life.

My father, William, was a former soldier from a working-class family in Highgate, North London. My mother, Patricia, was a daughter of the Empire born in Rangoon, Burma. As the 'Great War' in Europe was ending in 1918, she was growing up in Mamyo and Mandalay. Her family packed her off to boarding School in Ealing, West London when she was eight years old.

My mother was a beautiful woman with a mane of glossy black hair. She protected her milky-white porcelain features from the eastern sun with parasols and large picture hats. She wore lavender water but on special occasions she emitted the perfumed fragrance of Chanel No 5, a gift from her mother that lasted her about five years at a time. She wore face powder, rouge, eye mascara, eyebrow pencil and bright red lipstick on her cupid-shaped lips, reflecting the fashion of the day.

When she was seventeen, a magazine representative asked my mother to pose for their fashion pages but her father considered it unseemly. At the same time she met my father, a dashing young sergeant major, at a regimental dance in Burma. After a whirlwind romance she accepted his marriage proposal sent by telegraph and set sail on the P&O liner *SS Ganges* bound for Calcutta. She married Regimental Sergeant Major W. H. Bridgman in Lucknow, India on the 18th February 1936, only two months short of her eighteenth birthday.

My father, William Henry Bridgman, one of seven children, was born in Highgate on 1st December 1906. While my mother didn't lace her own shoes until she was eight years old because that was the privilege of her servant, my father didn't even *have* a pair of shoes. His first shoes were roughly carved wooden clogs which my grandfather made. My father's poor feet suffered and his bunions and hammer toes burdened him through the rest of his life.

When Dad was seventeen, the post-war depression of the 1920s was well and truly underway. One cold winter's day, he and his friend Tom were so hungry they begged an apple from a local greengrocer on the Holloway Road. A sharp-eyed Army Recruitment Officer knew his job and he could see they needed a square meal rather than the bread and dripping they got every day.

He offered them a meal in exchange for mucking out the stables behind the local Army Recruitment Office and soon had them both signing up.

Eighteen was the minimum age, so Dad lied about how old he was. Record-keeping was clearly erratic. Almost thirty years later he left the Army with the rank of Captain after serving in Burma, India, Palestine and the Western Desert.

My father cut a handsome figure as a 6' 1" young man in his army uniform. He had a firm jaw, waxed moustache and brilliantined black hair. My mother thought this good-looking sergeant major was a great catch. He was also her way out from the stifling rigidity and claustrophobic atmosphere of her family. She wanted to have her own full, exciting family life.

Yet my mother always struggled to adapt to the loss of money and status she'd grown up with in the Far East. Colonials in the East had high status with servants to take care of their every need. They brought that sense of importance home with them in their minds, but it didn't fit with a post-war Britain that was broke and on its knees.

Immediately after his demob from the Army in 1946, my father worked at the Royal Mint, where he bounced coins off a small leather pad the size of a knuckle to listen to the ring the impact made so as to check the coin was correctly minted. After that he loaded wallpaper on to lorries at the Sanderson wallpaper factory in Perivale, West London. He only ever took one day off sick twice: once when he was knocked off his bike on the way to work and broke his kneecap; and the second time when he had a benign brain tumour removed.

My father probably never experienced affection and never learned how to show it. From as far back as I can remember he shook hands rather than hugging me at night when I was put to bed. He was distant for the whole of his life. His way of showing his love for us was by providing security via the money that fed and clothed us.

My mother struggled with their finances, finding creative ways of making food and clothing last. When I was an adult, my father told me how my mother often went without an evening meal because she couldn't afford to feed us all. It left me with an enormous respect for her and the women of her generation who held families together on a shoestring budget and always put the children first. Both my parents believed they deserved better than the poverty and the food rationing they experienced after the war. To this day I retain an indelible fear of being poor.

That belief drove me to work for myself from the age of twenty-seven when I was made redundant from a job in the travel industry. I vowed this would never happen again and decided I'd always have control over my career. Even when I was forced to liquidate my business many years later with huge personal debt and the possibility of losing my home, I stormed into the bank manager's office and demanded he give me more time. He did. My fear of lack taught me to fight for everything. That's what my father taught me.

I was the youngest of three siblings. But something tragic happened to my parents that shaped all of our lives before any of us were even born.

After their wedding in India my parents spent a short time in Burma where my father's regiment was posted. Their first child, Pamela, was born in London in 1939. Immediately after the birth the regiment and hence my family was posted to Palestine. Pamela was a normal, healthy baby until she was four months old and contracted what the army doctor told my mother was a cold. He prescribed some cold relief medicine and sent her home but twenty-four hours later Pamela died of undiagnosed pneumonia.

My mother was barely twenty, a child herself in a foreign land. There was no email or telephone then and she was devastated. She wasn't even able to bury her dead child. My parents were due to leave Haifa on a troopship three days later and no other ships were available for several weeks. My mother never even saw the headstone that was made for her beloved firstborn. Fifty years later I was the first and only member of the family to locate and visit the grave.

Just before he died, my father told me about being aboard the ship in the port of Haifa and searching high and low for my mother. He couldn't find her anywhere and he was desperate. But as the ship pulled away from out of the harbour he discovered a forlorn figure crouched between a funnel and a gunwale. It was my mother, sobbing uncontrollably as the ship pulled out of the harbour. It is an image that has haunted me ever since.

Mother had a terrible fear of losing another child. If my sisters and I so much as sneezed, we'd be whisked off to bed with a hot-water bottle to prevent a cold, which had barely manifested itself, from turning into the dreaded killer pneumonia.

My bedroom was a place with which I became well acquainted during my childhood. I was a sickly child and had endless bouts of tonsillitis, flu and just about every illness imaginable. I rarely went more than a couple of weeks without ending up in bed with a thermometer in my mouth. Just how much was down to genuine illness I will never know. For several months I received daily booster injections from Nurse Ratchet.

"Sorry, but this might hurt a bit," she'd say each time she fired the daily syringe into my buttocks.

When I was six, I had scarlet fever and was laid low for several weeks. And after a visit to Ealing Swimming Baths my older sister Geraldine (later known as Dina) and I contracted polio. If you were very lucky, your stiff aching limbs returned to normal. The doctor told my mother if my temperature didn't go down by the fourth morning, I would have to be admitted to hospital. During the night I woke up to find my mother kneeling at my bedside with her hands clasped tight and her head bowed in prayer. God needed to listen to her. And apparently He did. By morning my temperature had subsided and I could start moving my arms and legs.

Polio left me with a very slight distortion of my right elbow joint, which afforded me the opportunity to entertain friends and relatives by bending it inwards to the accompaniment of groans from my audience. Was this the beginning of my experience as an entertainer?

It was the Asian flu epidemic in the fifties that gave my mother the biggest scare. Like virtually everyone else in the country my sisters and I contracted this new strain of flu. In my case, the temperature stayed high. Weakened from years of illnesses I struggled to shake it off and it morphed into the dreaded pneumonia.

I can't imagine what went through my mother's mind. The mere utterance of that word *pneumonia* by the doctor must have instilled terror in her. There were more night-time prayers and endless glasses of orange juice. Again, my temperature subsided and I made a slow, but full, recovery. Again my mother thanked God. As ever, Dad was silent and stayed in the background.

But I wasn't sure I believed in this God of Love. He didn't seem to love *me* very much. If He loved me, why didn't He answer my prayers that begged him to make me normal?

This catalogue of illnesses meant that I missed a lot of school from the age of five to about eight. But it didn't matter to me because I hated it. I hated school almost as much as I hated my male body which was emaciated by my illnesses and my hatred of food. Those feelings began very early on in my life.

I never gave up on myself or had suicidal thoughts although I was constantly fearful and depressed.

As for my father, he just didn't know the meaning of the word *quit*. His favourite saying was, 'If at first you don't succeed, try, try, try again.' Sometimes I wish he'd added '…but change direction if things aren't working!'

Dad lived a life of hard graft. There was no welfare state then and days off were not an option. Neither his generation nor my own really learned that you could work *smarter*.

He was a man's man and I'm afraid his sickly, effeminate son was a big disappointment to him. In his later years when dementia robbed him of the ability to dislike me or be angry with me because of who I was, he opened up a little and told me stories about his boyhood.

Once he told me about a telegram boy delivering the news that one of his brothers was killed in action during the First World War. My grandmother said she couldn't stop work so she asked my father to run up to the Essex Road where my grandfather, himself wounded in the conflict and discharged was laying cobbles on the road, to deliver the news that their son was dead. My grandfather simply said, "Go back and tell your mum I'll try and leave work a bit early."

These were not the words of callous, uncaring parents but the communication of men and women who knew there would be no food on the table if they stopped work early.

My father was a working-class Tory in the days when Conservatives, Socialists and Liberals had very clearly defined remits for the people they represented. I think he believed voting Conservative would somehow deny the crushing poverty of his youth and convince himself that he really was superior and well-off.

When Asian and Caribbean immigrants arrived, he was happy to accept the need for these *inferior* people to do the jobs his generation didn't want to do. Cleaning toilets and driving buses and trains was not something a gentleman who had been part of the *victorious British Army* should be expected to undertake.

He greeted any talk of Gandhi or the first Prime Minister of India, Pandit Nehru, with 'damned terrorists'! It was only when I was older and read history for myself that I discovered British rulers weren't all covered in glory and quite as superior as I'd been brought up to believe.

My mother's mother, Granny Cooper, was a familiar face and a huge, lasting influence on me. She was a short woman with long grey hair tied in a bun and she looked like the granny in the Giles cartoons, which were popular in the Fifties and Sixties. She had a round face and rosy cheeks and an ability to find laughter in almost any situation.

Granny loved her food and in the heat of summer she often sat with me on her doorstep at the back of the house in Ealing, in her wrap-over pinafore laden with fruit from her fruit garden, eating her way through the Victoria plums and peaches she'd picked earlier in the day. Most of them failed to reach the cool of the larder.

"Just one more," we said to each other over and over until both of us were full to bursting when she'd say, "Your Mother'll kill me if you get an upset stomach!"

Colonialism can't be justified but whilst many colonials lorded it around the world with an air of superiority, Granny talked with fondness of the lovely people she knew and had lived with in India. She told me about inviting the 'dhobi wallah' (the servant who did the washing) in for afternoon tea and learning Hindi from her 'bearer' (personal servant). She learned the art of authentic Indian cooking and she gave me a love for curry from a very early age. Her tomato sambal, a hot-tasting chutney, was legendary in our family. It was a terrible shock when I heard Granny Cooper suffered a heart attack and died suddenly. She had been on holiday in Liverpool with Aunt Mercia. It was decided I wasn't old enough to attend the funeral so I stayed at home while my parents and sisters headed north. Parents never give children enough credit for their maturity in situations such as these and mine didn't understand my need to say goodbye. I feel my special Granny has remained with me on my journey. Her sense of humour and love of life has been a massive support to me in my darkest hours.

It was her love of laughter that I most remember about her and I must have inherited a love of comedy from somewhere. We loved The Goon Show. We used to listen to 'Take It From Here' written by Frank Muir and Dennis Norden and starring Jimmy Edwards, Dick Bentley, Alma Cogan and, in my opinion, the most underrated comedy actress of her or any other generation, June Whitfield. I particularly liked Tony Hancock with his morose, dry delivery. He was probably the only comic to successfully transfer from radio to television. His line from a show when he was responding to Sunday dinner served up by his landlady, Mrs Cravat, played by another brilliant comedy actress, Hattie Jacques, is my favourite one-liner from anywhere. In answer to her question, "What's wrong with the dinner?" he replied, "Well at least my mother's gravy used to move around the plate."

The word 'genius' is bandied about too much but Spike Milligan and Tony Hancock wouldn't have been embarrassed by the adjective. It also sits firmly on the shoulders of my third comedy hero, Groucho Marx. I only saw glimpses of the Marx Brothers when I was small, since going to the cinema was an expensive luxury. When I did see those old black and white movies, I was blown away by the anarchical humour and one-liners, only equalled by Milligan. The gift shared by Spike and Groucho was the ability to be even funnier in print than when performing, although they could do both almost as well. Hancock, Milligan and Groucho Marx all had their darker sides. Groucho had three failed marriages, Spike was constantly battling mental illness and depression, and Hancock took his own life in Australia, in the belief he was failing and unloved.

Does the humour emerge from their sadness or do they use laughter as a foil for their dark moments? I don't think all comics are pained souls looking for an outlet but I do know that laughter becomes more poignant and somehow richer when you've experienced sadness and isolation. I can't imagine a world without people who are brave enough to put themselves out there and risk rejection in the pursuit of sharing laughter. And I can still hear my granny's giggles.

My grandparents' house in Ealing was like a shrine to the Raj and the Empire with artefacts from all over India. They had beautiful teak coffee tables carved in the shape of an elephant, rugs, silk hangings from China and cork pictures from Hong Kong. A tiger-skin rug resplendent with head dominated the lounge floor.

When I read Kipling, I had the book propped up against the tiger's head. My granny told me stories of Durbars and tigers in India, of women in beautiful saris, brave Sikh warriors, the heat of the plains, cool evenings in Lucknow, and train journeys through magical lands. She sowed the seeds of my love of travel with her wonderfully colourful stories.

Her long garden in Ealing became my own magical land. It had beautiful aromatic roses with herbaceous borders surrounding emerald green lawns. A birdbath interrupted the gentle descent down to a fenced off fruit garden. In the summer holidays I played hide-and-seek with mythical friends and in the autumn I picked fruit from the peach, plum, apple, pear and cherry trees which protected the gooseberry and strawberry plants from the harsh sun of summer and the icy frosts of winter.

My grandfather had green fingers that produced glorious roses that stood like tall beacons throughout the garden. He refused to prune them. He said if God had created them, God would take care of them. Intoxicated by the summer scents, I competed with the bees to take in the aromas.

Here in this magical garden I wasn't Michael any more. And I wasn't 'Skinny Minnie' or 'Belsen' either — a cruel name they taunted me with at school, recalling the sickening images of the liberated prisoners from Nazi concentration camps. In my private garden in Ealing I was a princess wearing a crimson red satin ball-gown over full, frothy petticoats, my hair tied back with ribbons. Maybe, just maybe, when I grew up, I'd be pretty and have a slim figure with hips and small breasts and maybe I'd be allowed to wear pretty dresses and patent leather shoes.

Granny had an infectious laugh and would shake silently, rocking in the chair with tears of laughter streaming down her cheeks. Most of the time we had absolutely no idea what was tickling her. She was totally incapable of speech during these episodes. 'Granny's off' meant she was about to have a fit of her famous silent giggles.

Granddad worked in the War Office. On his return home in the early evening his prayer ritual would take place. We all knew to remain silent as he removed his hat and stood in the hallway in prayer at the foot of the stairs for four or five minutes. Only then could anyone speak to him. It was the same each morning as he prayed before leaving home.

He was a lay preacher in his local church and he was a daunting figure, not to be trifled with. My mother and grandmother respected him but there was always an element of fear. There was absolutely no doubt who was the master of the house even though it was granny who held everything together.

So it was that I grew up with a family fighting to adjust to life in England and find its identity. This too was my struggle.

From my first day at school I knew I was different from everyone else. It was at school that the social consequence of being treated as male became a real lived experience. I wanted to sit with the girls on their side of the room but they made me sit with the boys, who were busy banging wooden pegs into small wooden frames with holes in. Distressed and desolate, I ran home at break only to be marched back in tears. I repeated this exercise every day for a week. I hated school from that first morning and I hated it for the next ten years until I left at the age of fifteen.

"Why can't I be a girl and sit with the girls, Mum?" I used to ask my mother.

"You're a boy and boys have to sit together at school." It was always the same answer.

My mum and the vicar often reminded me that God created everything perfectly, including me. Even at that young age I knew something was desperately wrong. I was created by God but I was different to everyone else in the world. Why? Why, God? Why?

They told me I needed to have faith so I prayed that when I grew up and went to the senior school, I'd be a girl. I didn't know who else I could ask.

What was happening to me back then? Why was it happening? Was there a lesson I was supposed to be learning? What was my life purpose? These are questions we've all asked on our life journeys. It's just that I began asking them early on.

IMAGINARY CONVERSATIONS

"How important it is for us to recognize and celebrate our heroes and sheroes!"
Maya Angelou

When I try to make sense of it all, I also try to imagine what my heroes and sheroes might make of my experiences. I decided to ask them and have imaginary or virtual conversations with these great people who have inspired me. The voices are really my own, of course, and not theirs but I wondered what I could learn from them if I imagined how they might respond to my questions, to hear my voice spoken through them. Some of the words or phrases may have been written or spoken by them at one time or another but in a different context. Any words or phrases written or spoken by them and not attributed to them is unintentional.

IMAGINARY CONVERSATION WITH GRANNY COOPER

"Nobody can do for little children what grandparents do. Grandparents sort of sprinkle stardust over the lives of little children."
Alex Haley

I'm so sad I didn't connect more with you when I was growing up. It's only since you died and after becoming an adult that I began to appreciate how important you were then and still are to me now. Your sheer joy of life, your passion for food and love of people has inspired me throughout my life. I didn't fully realise at the time what a guardian angel you were and how much you supported my parents and helped us with money for food and clothes when times were hard.

Tell me what you think about how we connect with each other?

Well, what does connection mean? We make everything too complicated! Connection just means being open and fully accepting the people with whom we form relationships. The connection comes in the *trying*. We connect when we see the other person really trying to understand us and accept us for who we are, with all our gifts and all our failings. No judgements or preconditions, just acceptance. Child, what we do *with* and *for* others defines us as human beings. We don't live in a bubble, separate from the rest of the world. We *can't* live like that. You know from your own experience when you tried to be someone you weren't, it didn't work.

Yes, philosophers like Martin Buber talk about 'Presence' and 'I-Thou moments'. I think they're describing those special moments when our eyes and our souls connect and we feel fully met, even if it's just for a fleeting moment. In those moments we feel validated and alive.

Exactly. True friendship is about not imposing yourself on friends but making yourself available. There's a really important distinction. True friends don't try to fix you. True friends are the ones you can call at four a.m. when your heart's breaking.

I love Oriah Mountain Dreamer's definition of friendship when she says, "It doesn't interest me who you know or how you came to be here. I want to know if you'll stand in the centre of the fire with me and not shrink back."

Yes. Do you value the friend who's always asking you what you're doing and why and who's always telling you how to solve all your problems? No, you want the friend who's always there for you, always available, someone who'll stand next to you in the trenches while the war's raging around you and who doesn't flinch when the shells of life's problems explode around you. He or she is your true friend.

You were part of the colonial empire. I always wondered how you squared that circle as a woman who believed in people and their right to fulfilment?

Well, I was born into an unjust system although I didn't understand that at the time. Sometimes we work within the system we inherit and other times we have to change it. All unjust systems die in the end. They die because they're based on inequality and one party taking from the other, or thinking they're superior.

India got its independence because the natural order was restored. Communism faltered around the world because the ideals of Marx and Engels were distorted by dictators who sought control and power, rather than working for the very people who gave them that power. Apartheid ended because a system based upon inequality, control and fear is always doomed. The people who were discriminated against rose up to reclaim their country.

All of these revolutions were successful because they had freedom or love at the core.

You can't force connection. You can only open your heart to allow it in and hope that people feel it, don't you think? Then it has an amazing power of its own. Remember, child, power corrupts. Those who seek connection in a cynical manner as a route to power always lose that power once those who gave it to them realise they've been manipulated. Make yourself available to people with love and they'll find you.

What is it that makes some of us crave that connection while others prefer to be on their own?

Some of it we inherit through our genes, some of it through our learned experience. For some, solitude is positive but for others it's something they fear because they associate it with pain. In the end we all find a way of connecting or not connecting that's right for us and allows us to feel safe. The problem is that simply coping is not really living.

I think healing begins when we're connected and validated by others. That's why people devour self-help books, going from one to the other looking for magic answers in their quest for enlightenment. But I've realised we don't really learn deeply unless it's through experience and looking outside ourselves as well as inward reflection.

Yes, I think great teachers guide their pupils on journeys of self-discovery rather than sharing their great 'wisdom' as though they know better.

What would you advise those lost souls seeking connection?

Never stop. As Jesus said, "Seek and ye shall find." Don't give up on your journey because understanding is always closer than you think. It cannot be forced because we demand it. We have to allow it in. Remember, all actions created with love at its core will always be returned to you with love and you'll receive ten times more than you gave.

2
GROWING

"Difficulties come when you don't pay attention to life's whisper.
Life always whispers to you first, but if you ignore the whisper,
sooner or later you'll get a scream."
Oprah Winfrey

———————◦◦◦———————

Life in our *prefab* in Leemead Avenue was getting cramped. After two years on a council waiting list we were moved to Rushdene Crescent on the Northolt Grange Estate in Northolt, West London. It was 1950.

The Northolt Grange housing estate covered about a square mile of identical, semi-detached houses interspersed with a few flats or apartments with a long footpath dissecting the dozen or so roads and cul-de-sacs within it. Cars were a luxury only afforded by the wealthy and their almost total absence meant the footpath was the main access to the various dwellings that made up the estate.

Our three bedroom red brick semi-detached house had a small front garden framed by a low brick wall bordering the pavement. The long garden at the rear backed onto a similar property which faced yet another red bricked council house. There were no garages and no driveways but we shared a concrete path with next door which led to large sheds and a coal bunker. Although nobody owned their own car in our street, our neighbour parked his removal lorry outside his house. The only other vehicles in the street were another couple of commercial vehicles that other neighbours would bring home from their work.

Everyone took great pride in the appearance of their homes. The front and back gardens had small manicured lawns and meticulously kept flower beds. The last third of the back gardens were generally converted to vegetable patches. We planted two peach stones from Granny Cooper's garden in our back garden where they eventually grew to become huge trees which bore fruit for the majority of my childhood. Rationing for various commodities was still in force, mainly for sugar, candy and sweets. Vegetable growing was born out of necessity rather than choice.

My sisters, Penny and Geraldine, shared the rear bedroom, my parents had the double room at the front, and a small bedroom at the corner of the house became my sanctuary.

There was a reasonably sized kitchen with no appliances other than a gas stove and a mangle to remove the excess water from the laundry, which was washed by hand in the sink. The kitchen contained a large larder where perishable food was stored.

From the kitchen there was an arch leading to the dining room and living room and then into the front room or 'best' room which was reserved for visitors and guests. Both living rooms had fireplaces which backed on to the boiler, the source of our hot water.

A tiger skin rug adorned the middle of the living room in the front of the house. Mercifully it was without a head. It was our homage to the remnants of a shrinking Empire.

Every room had a picture rail with white emulsion painted above them and across the ceiling. Below the picture rails were the latest designs in wallpaper obtained on staff discount from Dad's place of work. We had the best and most contemporary wallpaper in Rushdene Crescent, probably in the whole of Northolt. I don't recall a single holiday when my father wasn't decorating one of the rooms in the house.

Bob and Edna were our next-door neighbours. They had two boys: Paul, a year older than me and Malcolm, a year younger. The boys were lively lads who were obsessed with taking their toys apart to see how they worked, much to the annoyance of their mother who was often heard bawling them out over the destruction of yet another mechanical toy. The highlight of their careers as budding engineers was when they launched a clock they were unable to reconstruct through the dining room window and onto the concrete patio where its life ended in an explosion of metal fragments.

Our neighbours on the other side were the Rohan family. The dad was a big gruff Irishman who worked for the Council. He kept chickens in his back garden. My mother complained about the smell in the summer and the noise of the crowing cockerel and clucking chickens in the winter. But she didn't complain when they regularly gave us eggs — and, on more than one Christmas, a chicken. Chicken was a luxury in those days and turkey was unheard of.

When I was very young Granny bought us a goose for Christmas, which was then routine Christmas fare. Presumably geese are relieved to have become less popular.

Michael was one of three boys and being my age, we became friends. His big brother Chris was a 'Teddy Boy' with greased-back hair, smart suits with velvet collars, bottle creeper suede shoes and 'drainpipe' trousers.

Michael's younger brother, Martin, was a slow developer who struggled with speech and was unable to form words until he was six or seven. He succumbed to leukaemia and died when he was only eight. I remember my mother consoling the family. Of course, she knew what it was like to experience such a loss. Their father was broken. It was the first time I'd ever seen a grown man cry.

Like most of the people in our street, our neighbours had a kind nature and would always be on hand to offer support when anyone needed it. They had all come through a terrible war and had stood together to defeat the Nazis. They were not about to abandon each other when a little challenge like lack of money presented itself.

My sisters were both much older than me. By the time I was five Geraldine was twelve and in senior school and Penny was sixteen. I had more in common with Geraldine. Despite the seven-year difference our birthdays were a day apart on 30th and 31st May, which probably accounts for our similar personalities. We were both fair-haired, loved humour and would drive everyone mad with our incessant impersonations of the various Goon Show characters. I was 'Bluebottle' to her 'Neddy Seagoon'.

Geraldine had to wear spectacles from an early age. Her sight problems were perhaps caused by my mother having a bout of German measles while she was pregnant. Geraldine's eyesight probably wasn't helped by the fact that she was always reading. She was known as the family bookworm and we both inherited our mother's love of literature. Geraldine was never without a book in her hand. She averaged roughly two books a week throughout her entire life.

Penny, on the other hand, was the dark-haired one. Always quiet and serious, it was Penny who helped my mother in the kitchen or went out shopping with her. "Why can't you be more like Penny?" my mother used to ask Geraldine and me whenever we were scolded for talking back or not doing exactly as we were told. We both had an element of the rebel in us.

We all got on well together but I never felt I had very much in common with Penny. It wasn't such a shock when she distanced herself from me years later when my actions made her ashamed of me.

When I was about eight, my dad bought me a red plastic football, which I would kick up against the wall of the coal bunker for hours at a time. My dad was always talking about football and his beloved Tottenham Hotspur. I decided I needed a different team to support.

The first game I ever saw was on Granny's television. I was nearly eight when Manchester City played Birmingham City in the FA Cup Final in 1956. It became famous because the Manchester City goalkeeper, Bert Trautmann, injured his neck but had carried on playing only to discover after the game that it was broken. How he survived without paralysis is a miracle.

The next Cup Final was between Manchester United and Aston Villa. United usually wore red, my favourite colour. Better still, they had won the FA Cup in the year I was born. They became the underdogs when their goalkeeper, Ray Woods, was injured. I liked underdogs.

They lost the game but I told the boys at school that I supported them. I had my team.

Football became my ticket to some sort of acceptance by my peers. I was struggling to be like the other boys and I hoped it might help me. We played football for hours at a time on the road outside the house. The kerbs were the touchlines and the thin strips of tar across the sections of the concrete road were the goal lines at either end. The goalposts were screwed up jackets or pullovers.

Our long-suffering parents complained they had no money to purchase replacements for our scuffed shoes. All of us wore shoes that had been bought a size bigger than needed so we could grow into them but the soles wore out long before then. Holes, however, were not a good enough reason to discard a perfectly good pair of shoes. Our parents would cut out inner soles from breakfast cereal packets and replace them on a daily basis as they wore out. We had a bizarre hierarchy of children comparing the quality of their cardboard inner soles.

In summer we converted the lines across our road to the lines of a tennis court, with one section of road acting as no man's land and doubled as an alternative to a net. Our hands were ready-made tennis rackets. If the weather was bad, we would retreat indoors and indulge in endless Monopoly fests. I never understood the strategy of buying cheap and building up capital. I always ignored Old Kent Road and waited until I landed on the prestigious upper-class Park Lane or Mayfair. It's not a strategy that's served me very well in life. It smacks of people relying on that lucky break in the lottery as the only means of attaining wealth.

At the age of eight the doctors eventually decided that my constantly inflamed tonsils needed removing. The only problem was there was a two-year waiting list. Seeing the despair in my mother's eyes, Granny Cooper came to the rescue yet again and delved into her savings. The sum of £20 got me into the Hillingdon Cottage Hospital which was then a small private hospital. My offending tonsils were removed and after gallons of ice cream which, along with fruit, was my favourite food by a mile, I returned home to improved health. It was a turning point in my life. For the first time I could participate fully in school without missing lessons and needing to be catching up all the time.

Although my tonsil operation was done privately, my healthcare and that of my counterparts would have been far poorer without the National Health Service. Whilst kicking a football around was about as macho as it got for me, I somehow contrived to break my arm on several occasions. Usually it was piggyback fights where one person would climb on his or her partner's back. The aim was to defeat your opponent by pulling the other person on top to the ground. Gender was never an issue as the girls were every bit as tough as the boys when it came to dislodging an opponent.

I had a good tolerance of pain. And there was a logical reason for that. By the age of eight I'd developed a technique of disassociating myself from my body to avoid the pain of the mismatch with my mind. It also served to help me deal with physical pain. One summer afternoon I was playing with my sister Geraldine when I tripped and fell on a broken milk bottle and gashed my knee. When I tried to walk, the gash widened and exposed my kneecap. My sister fainted and I carried her on my back the two hundred yards to home while blood streamed down my leg and into my socks and shoes. Several stitches and a tetanus jab later, I was running around once more.

I'm not sure when it was that I grudgingly gave up on the idea that I could grow up and be a girl. It was probably after that first traumatic day at school. Deep down I knew my body could never change but the thought that it was impossible to live as a female was just too awful to contemplate.

Over time I adapted to my life as a skinny, effeminate little boy. The words *pansy* and *sissy* were hurled at me a lot. They hurt me but I knew they didn't adequately describe me and what I was feeling. Even at the age of seven or eight I knew that this was not about me being a feminine boy, but about me really being a girl. It had all gone wrong somewhere. Had I done something to annoy God? Was it a birth defect? Was I really baby Pamela come back in another body? My first inkling that I may not be the only person on the planet who felt like me occurred on a holiday in Liverpool.

I was about seven years old when during a stay with my aunt and uncle I saw an article in the Sunday People newspaper about a man who'd changed to a woman. I was fascinated by it. I felt a scary connection with the story. I read it over and over and I remember dropping the paper like a hot potato when my mother entered the room, as though she might read my thoughts and know I really was different. It never occurred to me that I might one day be able to go through such a process.

Some gay men have told me they knew they were different from an early age. They understood their feelings for older boys were seen as 'unnatural'. I often wonder if homophobia in schools unwittingly extends to children with gender identity issues and if these children still slip through the net in that fashion. But that's another story.

I think I was nine years old when I first wore my sister's yellow dress. It was a school holiday and Mum had just popped next door for a few minutes. I found myself in my sisters' bedroom and I opened their large built-in double wardrobe to be confronted by a rail of skirts and dresses. Penny had a short-sleeved, lemon coloured gingham dress with a scoop neck, back zip, an A line skirt and a full petticoat. Very 1950s.

I had an uncontrollable urge to take the dress from the rail and put it on. Carefully I undid the back zip and, having quickly taken off my shorts and shirt, slipped into the dress. It was too big for me, so it was easy to do the back zip up at the front and then twist the dress round before putting my arms into the sleeves. The waistband did up at the back with several hooks and eyes but that felt too risky. I knew my mother would come back soon and I could only manage to take it off in time if I left them undone.

When I saw myself in the mirror, I wept tears of joy. I looked pretty and the dress was beautiful. But within seconds the joy turned into shame and fear. I was now officially weird. In a flash I removed the dress and replaced it on its hanger and re-dressed in my own clothes. As my mother returned, I ran past her telling her that I was going out to play. I ran and ran. I ran along the street, round the Crescent and down to the open fields which led to the West London Shooting Grounds. And I kept running. It was almost as though I was trying to get away from myself. I sat down on a log in the fields and sobbed. My 'problem' was now confirmed.

I repeated that episode with the dress many times over in the next couple of years. Seizing a few minutes alone I would creep into the bedroom and wear the dress for one or maybe two minutes, just enough to remind myself what I looked like. We'd had dressing up games as kids and I'd played with my Mother's makeup until she scolded me, but this was different. This was me expressing myself as I really wanted to and I felt a powerful cocktail of emotions every time. I was both elated and ashamed. I was terrified I might be found out. The pattern repeated itself over and over. Anticipation, joy and relief followed by shame and self-loathing. Deep down I think I knew I had let the genie out of the bottle and it would never go back.

It's often said that people are trapped in the wrong body. I've never quite seen it like that because I wasn't deluded. I'd come to realise I wasn't a girl and that I wasn't destined to be a girl. But it didn't stop me feeling that I should have been one. I was an unhappy little boy harbouring a dark secret. I just didn't know how I'd cope with my feelings. I prayed I'd grow up quickly and leave childhood behind.

One of the neighbour's boys, although he didn't know it, would give me the tools to at least cope with my life as a boy. Brian was everything I wasn't. He was strong, confident and he mixed well with the other boys in the road, even if they were a little intimidated by him. I can't remember how it started but I became his chosen target, a victim of his bullying. Like all bullies there was a cowardly streak in him and I was an easy prey. At first it was just name-calling just like he did with all the other children, but then it evolved into threats of violence, and then violence itself.

Brian used to steal my apple or peach or whatever I took into school. If anyone challenged him, he'd say I'd agreed to let him have it. In fear of reprisal I'd meekly comply and confirm his story. Then he started knocking books out of my hand and making me carry his satchel. Chinese burns on the arm or punches in the back that didn't show were all part of his repertoire.

My only defence was to try and avoid him. It isn't just one event that's so upsetting. It's the cumulative effect of systematic abuse which is so debilitating. But what made it worse was that his father witnessed some of this behaviour and saw it as his macho little boy growing up and becoming masculine.

And it wasn't just against me. On one particular occasion on a summer afternoon, Brian turned his attention to a boy called Roy. Roy and I weren't friends but I knew his face from school. He suffered from some form of epilepsy or petit mal and had blackouts and seizures. Brian often walked with me to school on the pretence that we were friends and then he'd taunt me and goad me into being his boxing sparring partner. If I declined, he'd push me around to try and provoke a response. On this particular occasion Roy witnessed this bullying and intervened.

"Leave him alone. He's too weak," he said.

Brian turned his attention to Roy and after an exchange of words the punches started to fly. A crowd of kids circled the two protagonists with boys showing their allegiance by cheering. It wasn't long before Brian got the better of Roy and got on top of him, pinning his shoulders to the ground with his knees.

Roy's face was reduced to a bloody mess as the blows rained down and he couldn't shield himself. But he refused to give in. The most sickening aspect of the whole spectacle was when Brian's mother arrived on the scene. Instead of intervening she complimented her son and suggested to Roy that he 'admit defeat' so the punishment would stop.

At this point Roy's nose exploded into a streaming red mess and the crowd of boys who'd been baying for blood realised the extent of the beating and fell quiet. Only then did the victor realise he was in danger of going too far and stopped.

"Let this be a warning to the rest of you!" his proud mother warned us all as they left the scene.

Looking back on the responses of his parents, it's no surprise Brian was a bully. Who knows what nightmares of his own he had as a child? But at the age of nine I didn't speculate on his background and the experiences fuelling his aggression. My own survival was paramount.

I walked home after this incident and felt utter despair at my impotence in protecting myself and shame for standing by while someone who tried to protect me took a terrible beating as a result of his courage. He was doubly brave in standing up for me and then for refusing to admit defeat.

I went upstairs and crawled under my bed before crying uncontrollably. A seed was planted in me that day. I vowed to change my life although I didn't know how.

The answer was just around the corner outside the school gates.

One of Brian's habits was to intercept me at the school gates and walk along taunting me. A few weeks after the incident with Roy he decided to humiliate me in front of the other children. He invited me to spar with him and raised his fists in the usual boxing stance. When I refused, he threatened to 'beat me up'.

It may seem remarkable to anyone not around in 1950s Britain but fighting was very much a case of hitting back rather than openly attacking and striking the first blow, which was seen as unwarranted aggression. Fights like the one with Roy would begin with pushing and shoving before any blows were thrown. Brian stood there goading me to fight him while the swelling crowd urged me to run. They shouted, "Run or he'll kill you!"

But something snapped inside me and I stood firm. I had had enough. He might kill me but I was finished with running.

"I'm not running anywhere," I said, as I held his gaze. His smile turned to a weak grin. He carried on taunting me but he knew the entire school would see him as a cowardly bully if he hit 'skinny Minnie'. Roy fought him but I wasn't fighting him. I just wouldn't back down. For the first time in my life I realised I had power.

This standoff continued for fifteen or twenty minutes before Brian uttered something about not wasting time with a scrawny runt like me and walked away. Over the following weeks and months he called me names, but the violence stopped. He moved on to someone else and I was free of my tormentor. This new experience of being still and at one with myself would be repeated many years later on the shore of Lake Titicaca in South America, when I would again find strength and peace after life-threatening violence.

Around a year later a boy named Peter told me he was joining Hayes Boxing Club and invited me to go along with him. I was scared by the prospect but reasoned that if I was going to survive it might be worth a try.

Hayes Amateur Boxing Club was run by a legendary trainer called Dick Gunn who went on to train Chris Finnegan, winner of a gold medal at the Mexico Olympics in 1968, before a long and successful professional career. The club was very macho but it was also scrupulously fair. On the rare occasion that two boys fell out or sparring was over-enthusiastic, a whistle would blow, the trainer would throw the gloves at the offending parties and get them in the ring for three rounds of boxing followed by a warning that they'd be expelled from the club if it was repeated. At the end of the fight they'd be made to shake hands.

I felt like a foreigner in the gym but to my surprise I discovered I could actually box. What I lacked in physical strength I made up for in technique by moving quickly and having fast hands. My opponents may have been tougher but at the age of eleven I was nearly six feet tall and that gave me a longer reach. This with my fast hands and feet made it difficult for my opponents to land blows.

In secondary school I went on to become a Middlesex (how appropriate that seems) County Champion although I only won on a bye as my opponent failed to make the weight in the final.

Around the same time I was picked to represent the Hayes club in a competition with a club from another area. I was in my smart black and gold shorts and canvas plimsolls because proper boxing boots were too expensive. My opponent was a lad in scruffy old shorts and plimsolls but he was really tough and would have none of my dancing round the ring. He waded through my jabs and hooks and got through my defences. Although it was a close contest, he defeated me on points.

Trainer Dick said I ought to do more work with weights if I wanted to make it as a boxer. That was the death knell of my boxing career because I didn't want big muscles and so I declined the invitation. Shortly afterwards I discovered judo, a sport I loved which was more reliant on technique than brawn. My career as a boxer was over and I took up judo at the Ealing Youth Judo Club.

Training sessions or Randori, as they were called in Japanese, were fun but exhausting. On frequent visits to the Budokwai Club in London we trained with top-notch practitioners and lost up to five or six pounds in body fluid during a training session. Judo has to be the best sport for all-round fitness.

There was another benefit. Judo taught me to reconnect with my body and while I still hated it, I found something that helped me respect it and I began to take greater care of it. I even began to enjoy food. As the years have rolled by, I've enjoyed it rather too much.

With my improved health I got better marks at school. I hated Maths and History but I loved English and Geography. It's a great indictment of teaching methods in the fifties that I only grew to love History after I'd left school. The Industrial Revolution had bored me rigid. I knew the world extended beyond Calais but my history teachers apparently didn't.

To say I loved Geography isn't strictly true. I had an absolute passion for looking at maps and atlases. As a sickly child my mother bought me jigsaw puzzles of countries and continents. By the age of ten I knew not just the capital cities of most countries but the ports that served them as well. I won bets in the playground naming capitals and ports.

My problem with school was that I hated the environment. Teachers were strict. One word spoken out of turn resulted in a visit to the Head. With some teachers it led to a flogging with a slipper in front of the class. We were in class 2 and that meant we were not bright kids. Our class teacher told us we were not clever enough for grammar school.

When I sat down to do the eleven-plus exam, I was faced with Maths questions on topics we'd never covered. The English section was easier but we were all destined to fail. There were feelings of frustration and anger amongst my classmates. Our complaints went unheard and I was duly assigned a place at Vincent Secondary Modern School in Northolt.

It was further than Walford Secondary, where many of the children from the junior school were going but my sisters had been to Vincent and I was happy to have a new start, maybe a chance to make new friends.

Classes were now called forms and I was assigned a place in Form 1B. My Form Teacher was a formidable woman named Miss Tombes. She developed an instant liking or hatred of certain children. I fell somewhere in between the two polarities and managed to disappear within the class. One poor lad called Ray was not so lucky. He was constantly criticised and told off because his work wasn't up to scratch. What became of him I don't know but his confidence must have been sorely affected. It was teaching at its worst.

School was a fearful place. The slipper had graduated to the cane and boys as well as the occasional girl were subjected to corporal punishment on a daily basis. In the 21st century we call this child abuse, which is exactly what it was. In the third term I became one of Miss Tombes' hated children and received the same diatribe of criticism that others had endured earlier in the year. Luckily for me it was a short term and it was all over quickly.

Sport came to my rescue. Aside from boxing in that first year I was picked for the football team and we won the 'Minors' Cup beating Little Ealing School who had won the league. I was an old-fashioned right half wearing a number 4. From this position I was the link between defence and attack, although I was known as a fierce tackler.

We had a formidable halfback line with the tough Randy at number 5 and our Captain, Rob, the number 6. On a football pitch thoughts of lemon-coloured dresses, bullies and horrible teachers could be set aside for a while. Here I was equal to everyone else.

My school report said, "Makes up for limited ability by having a 'Never Say Die' Attitude." I didn't like the limited ability bit but I was pleased I'd inherited my Dad's attitude to life. I knew it was a trait that would serve me well.

School studies began to fall by the wayside as I could see no relevance to most of the subjects and in secondary school we knew we had little chance of going on to do 'A' levels. Added to which, if you were bright and got good marks, you were teased by the other kids. I decided it was much better to do well at sport and be accepted by my peers. If it hadn't been for sport, I think I would have gone crazy.

When winter turned to spring, football and boxing were replaced by cricket and athletics. I loved the long jump and high jump. I later idolised the East German long jumper, Heike Drechsler, reasoning that any woman who was 6 feet tall and as talented and beautiful as she was couldn't be all bad. To this day the women's long jump and high jump are my favourite Olympic sports.

There was one subject where not trying was not an option. Mr Fox, the Maths teacher, was a disciplinarian par excellence. Even fidgeting in class resulted in a reprimand. The toughest kids were fearful of a man who wasn't afraid to use the cane if he felt the behaviour warranted it. On day one we were told that no excuses for failing to hand in homework would be accepted. I hated Maths and I was petrified of Mr Fox. Double Maths on a Monday was the low point of the week.

The only subject I hated more than Maths was Physics. I went on to hold the unenviable record of having the lowest ever mark of 4 per cent in my mock GCE exam. However, by this point I had already decided that I would leave school at the earliest opportunity. I hated it with a passion and saw no point in staying any longer than I had to.

In secondary school my voice broke and I was beginning to turn from boy to man. The primal experience of feeling feminine had never gone away but I'd successfully suppressed it for much of the time. Puberty brought on a new challenge as my body began to change. Like most children of my generation, the 'Facts of Life' were largely uncovered in the playground at school. My father's idea of the 'Birds and the Bees' discussion consisted of giving me an illustrated booklet named 'Men and Women'. He handed it over with the words, "Your Mother thinks you should read this."

I'm not exactly sure what I expected from puberty. The notion of my sexuality was a strange concept. Whilst I'd always had the desire to be female, I'd never had any desire to have sexual contact with another boy. I liked girls and wanted to spend more time with them but I hadn't anticipated I might be sexually attracted to them.

When I reached puberty, I wondered if I'd become attracted to boys but I never was. In a sense that was even more confusing because I hadn't yet made the distinction between sexuality and gender. It's still a confusing aspect of transgender issues. People with gender identity issues are not necessarily gay men or lesbian women. Gender is a profound experience of identity and has little to do with sexuality.

When I was fourteen, I had a crush on Carole, a girl from school. I fantasised that she might like me and was horrified when she dated another boy from my class. I didn't want to have sex with her, I just wanted to be with her and share my life with her. Oh, the pain of a youthful infatuation! My desire to be female was still present but Carole and I could work it out. True love could overcome anything and this was true love. Inevitably, my passion passed and to this day the lovely Carole has absolutely no idea that I was madly in love with her.

IMAGINARY CONVERSATION WITH MR GANDHI

"Even if you are a minority of one, the truth is the truth."
Mohandas Mahatma Gandhi

My parents used to talk about this awful Mr. Gandhi who got rid of the British from India with another man called Nehru. According to my father they were terrorists and enemies of the Great British Empire. Worse still, they weren't Christians and they didn't believe in God.

Mahatma Gandhi died just a few months before I was born. But who was he really? Far from being a terrorist, I discovered he preached non-violence and only wanted us British to leave India because it belonged to India and not to Britain. Perhaps my parents had got this bit wrong? Did I have some of his spirit in me? After all Hindus believe in reincarnation, so his spirit had to go somewhere!

This funny little man was like me in the sense that he was *different*. Like me, he was skinny although unlike me, he wore a white loincloth over his frail frame. He wore funny glasses and carried a wooden staff. Perhaps he'd understand what creation is. So I asked him about it.

Were you happy as a child?

Well, I remember feeling loved but I'm not sure I understand your question. Hardship of any description is only experienced as a comparison to what we perceive to be better or easier. I understand you were unhappy with the body you were given, but it was part of your learning experience.

I was brought up with religion but I didn't find spirituality as a child. You seem to be very spiritual. Were you brought up with religion?

I too was brought up to be religious. When I was a child, we read from the Gita or the Koran. We didn't worry about only one being right. It only mattered that we worshipped God.

But who is God?

God is the Ultimate Creator. … the Architect of the Universe and the Constructor of Souls. Your soul yearns to grow closer to your creation and the Creator. True faith is when you believe in yourself enough to remain committed to your purpose. If you search for it, you'll find your purpose because your purpose is to bring yourself closer to God.

But how will I find my purpose?

Your life may be a long journey and you may sometimes feel lost but you have to trust the road even when it's bumpy, shrouded in mist and you're unsure of the way. You have to stop worrying about where the journey will finish. It's important to let go of the outcome and stay with the process of living. You need faith because you need to live and to learn from your life experience. If you lived in the knowledge of the outcome, you'd learn nothing.

So it is about the journey!

Of course. Your life is not the sum of one final experience. You're not working toward one fantastic final act. The value will be in the sum of your deeds and the lives you touch.

But why did I choose this life experience? I didn't want to be different.

You didn't choose it but you, like all of us, have something important to share with the world.

What is that?

That's your life's purpose. To go on your journey, to do it and to find out. To use the gifts you were given and find an activity or occupation that uses your gifts. Your purpose is to be the best you can be. Life offers abundant opportunity if we have a thirst for knowledge. Let go of the need to know the end result or you'll miss your learning on the journey.

You had so much to offer. Why was your life cut short by a man with a gun?

Because I'd achieved my life's purpose.

Does that mean I'll die when I've fulfilled my purpose?

No, child, not necessarily. But if you've chosen your path and if it's worthwhile, it's a difficult one. You may ruffle some feathers and upset some people. They may even attack you but you'll feel alive. Would you rather be ignored and achieve nothing? To please everyone would mean to give up on a part of yourself. Remember though that when you're at peace with yourself, people will be drawn to you. It's not inevitable that you'll be hated or attacked but if you are, know that you must be making a difference. If all your actions are based in love, you will attract far more love than hate.

Wise words. But how will I know when I've achieved what God wanted me to do?

When your parents created you in love, you began your journey and your journey will take you back home to *you*. You began your journey close to God. You moved away and then sought a way back home. When you've achieved that, then you'll be at one with God. Then you'll have truly fulfilled your life's purpose.

That makes it sound like such a long journey.

It is not always easy but when you stop living in the future and just stay in the present, your life force will be freed to enable your passage along the great river of life.

I began by asking you if you were happy as a child. What does true happiness mean?

What is happiness? Happiness is relative. To the starving child, a drop of her mother's milk is like nectar from God. To the wealthy financier, material trappings are the Holy Grail. Will the child stay satisfied for long? Will the person chasing monetary wealth be joyful for long? It's the thirst and hunger for knowledge, happiness and life's longing for itself that motivates us, but our connection with the Great Unseen is what we really crave. When we reach out, we begin to find our life's purpose. When we reach out to share the gifts we've been given, we step into our flow. Then and *only* then do we find our life's purpose. Only then will our hand be taken and guided on our journey home. Then we will have real wealth and abundance beyond measure. Remember while we're here, it is only by staying present and living at one with our bodies that we'll know true happiness.

3
CONNECTING AND BECOMING

*"Without friends no one would choose to live,
though he had all other goods."*
Aristotle

I set aside fantasies of being female and resolved to buckle down to work at being one of the boys. Secondary school gave me a chance to make new friends and start a new school life. The school was at the other end of Northolt, twenty minutes away by bus or an hour's walk. In the summer Peter, Roy (the recipient of the beating and now friend) and I would save the bus fare of three pence and buy instead a frozen Jubbly which was an orange drink in a prism-shaped carton. To the connoisseur a Jubbly always tasted far better when it was frozen solid and had to be sucked from its cardboard home. One Jubbly lasted long enough to sustain us on the walk to school. As we were all footballers in the same team, we often ran to improve our stamina.

During my second year at Vincent I was tipping over into adolescence and puberty. Gone were the short trousers which singled out the first year boys from the rest of the school. In came charcoal grey slacks worn with a black blazer featuring the school emblem of a silver eagle. It was a mixed school and the girls had their own entrance and playground. Not for them the grey and black. They had a burgundy uniform that was unflatteringly called maroon.

I found it increasingly harder to motivate myself for lessons but endless hours of boxing had given me status with the hard men of the school. Most of them were bigger and stronger and they knew they could take me apart if they felt like it but they respected me for being in the game. I was also a regular in the football team which was successful, either winning leagues or finishing runners-up. My status as one of the 'boys' was assured.

Then aged twelve, I was faced with the first great and unwelcome change in my life. My voice broke and hairs began to grow on my face. Surely this was further evidence that I was becoming a man and could put this girl thing behind me. My skinny frame had filled out a bit. I was still Skinny Minnie but now the name was used without any great malice.

My sexuality never came into question in my own mind. I found myself taking more and more notice of the girls, who were sprouting breasts and wearing skirts that showed off their shapely hips and legs.

A lovely girl named Shirley had the misfortune to have the biggest breasts in the entire school. They were big to the point where she was embarrassed by the comments and teasing they evoked from the boys. I think Shirley was torn between enjoying her journey into woman-hood and her assets which affirmed her femininity on the one hand and the unwelcome sexist comments from the boys on the other. Barely into her teens and still a child, she had no experience of handling the opposite sex and clearly became bored with the constant teasing. She was an attractive girl who just happened to develop physically ahead of her peers. I wanted to ask her what it felt like to have large breasts but the question would have been rude and worse still she might ask why a boy would want to ask what it felt like to have them rather than leering at them.

I'd always found it easier to talk to girls and had several girl friends with whom I spent time discussing fashion and music. The only three topics of any interest to most of my peers were clothes, music and sport. For the boys you could add sex and put it at the top of the list.

The girls were no doubt just as obsessed but sadly I wasn't privy to their discussions.

During my upbringing, talk of sex was suppressed. Other than the booklet my father handed me and schoolboy jokes, I had little knowledge of the 'facts of life' as they were known, and much of what I did know was pretty inaccurate. My first experience of even seeing pictures of men and women performing sexual acts was in my first year at Vincent when a large crowd gathered around one of the older boys in the playground who'd acquired a porn magazine. I remember about twenty boys huddling around Randy, an aptly named lad, who was the owner of the magazine.

"I recognise that face," said Geoff, the school swot to hoots of derisory laughter.

"Trust you to look at the face when two naked people are shagging," said Randy.

"No, look it's that tart from the dentist!" Geoff continued defensively.

The recognition of one of the naked models as the receptionist at the local dental surgery caused a great deal of amusement. Whether it was a coincidence or not, she left the dental practice shortly afterwards.

I remember finding it impossible to relate to these men performing acts on women. The thought of my body looking remotely like those men in the photographs was a distressing and alienating prospect.

Puberty is a confusing time for any young person. For me it was the final confirmation that I was destined to live with a body that was alien to my felt experience. My voice began to crack and deepen and wispy hairs grew on my face. And there was nothing I could do about it. I just had to get on with it. By now I was aware that there were people called hermaphrodites who were part male and part female but that was all I knew. Aside from the newspaper article I'd read on holiday in Liverpool I had no other reference and assumed nobody else on the planet felt the way I did.

Like all teenagers, I sought an identity. I loved music and had grown up through the fifties on a diet of rock 'n' roll. My neighbour Michael's brother, Chris, was the archetypal Teddy boy and he was always up with the latest music, which was usually from the USA and the Billboard charts. My sister Penny was into England's hero, Cliff Richard. I think *Living Doll* was the first 45 vinyl record to enter our house.

My mother had a large collection of 78s including a complete set of Al Jolson records which she adored. My favourite as a small child was Noel Coward's *Mad Dogs and Englishmen* which was only rivalled by Glenn Miller's *In the Mood*. I recall that Peter Sellers requested Glenn Miller's classic piece for his funeral. Peter's pals, Harry Secombe and Spike Milligan, enjoyed a wry smile when they heard it being played at the service because they knew their friend hated it with a passion. Even in death Sellers was cracking gags. Brilliant!

My older sister, Geraldine, bought a Dansette gramophone player which she'd saved up to buy from her first pay cheques when she started working.

The first record I bought was from a deal on the back of a cornflake packet. It was *What do you want make those eyes at me for?* by Emile Ford. This was followed by John Leyton's *Johnny Remember Me* before he went on to a film career which included a role in the classic movie *The Great Escape*. Every generation of young people identifies with a particular genre of music and looks to find heroes. Before the Second World War it was Swing, in the fifties Bill Haley introduced rock 'n' roll. Elvis Presley flaunted his sexuality, gave young men a role model to aspire to and sent women crazy. He was a far cry from the dinner-suited performers of the past. His behaviour provoked horror among parents and teenagers loved it. My generation was eager to break free of the austerity and conventional behaviours that typified the post-war years when nations had to pull together. I was not a teenager in the fifties and I didn't really identify with Elvis or the Teddy boy look but I did love the look for girls, typified by my sister's lemon dress.

By the time I was fourteen, young people were demanding more freedom and more choices. The old Conservative Party political order with Macmillan and then Alex Douglas-Home made way for Harold Wilson's new look Labour Party. Rock 'n' roll was not our music and we wanted a genre and style we could call our own. I remember sitting in the lounge when I first heard *Love Me Do* on the radio by a band (group as they were known then) called the Beatles. It was October 1962.

The song just had something special about it that was hard to define. It was new and fresh. And the boys had a new and distinctive look with round-collared suits that became known as Beatle Jackets. Their long mops of hair seemed short when compared to the hairstyles that followed but they really bucked the short back and sides crew cut trend, a throwback to military haircuts with slicked back hair. I rushed out and bought the single the very next day and everything they recorded ever since.

Shortly after the Beatles exploded on the scene, the buzz went round our class at school that a really amazing guy was playing at a coffee bar in Harrow. A classmate named Douggie burst into the Physics lab where we were assembling for a lesson.

"Hey, you seen who is on at the Kika Joo (a coffee bar in the nearby town of Harrow)? Donovan's on this Friday. Do you fancy it?"

I'd heard Donovan, who was being championed as Britain's Bob Dylan. Whilst I wasn't particularly keen on him, I wasn't about to pass up an opportunity to hear live music.

"I'm in," said I.

"Me too!" said three others in unison including Terry Burton, a boy with slicked-back hair.

"Piss off, Burton," said Douggie. "This isn't for Greasers. Put some Castrol on your hair and f.... off down the Ace!" (The Ace was a bikers' cafe on the North Circular Road in North London.)

Watching Donovan was the first time I'd seen a musician playing guitar, singing and playing the harmonica simultaneously. Best of all he sang songs for our generation, not someone else's.

Another time we went to see a group of guys with long hair at the Railway Hotel in Wealdstone; a group of bad boys led by a charismatic lead singer called Mick Jagger. With his gyrating hips and raw sex appeal he was the talisman for a generation. If Donovan and the Beatles had been trailblazers, the Rolling Stones were revolutionaries whom no parent would approve of.

We would go anywhere to watch the Stones. With them it was definitely as much about the performance as the music. The Beatles and the Rolling Stones were inspired by American Blues and in particular the R&B legend, Chuck Berry. I loved it … and I loved everything about the music scene.

A new look was taking hold. Beatle Jackets were quickly followed by something I found more exciting. My South London cousins Barry, Robin and Pauline were always up to speed with the latest developments in music and fashion. Pauline appeared one day wearing a blue nylon raincoat and with Hush Puppies on her feet. The look described kids who were 'Moderns' which quickly became abbreviated to 'Mods'. And it was for both boys *and* girls.

As an antidote, kids that didn't like the look or the 'poofy' music as they put it, preferring rock 'n' roll, became 'Rockers'. Where I lived everyone was a Rocker but it just wasn't me. Leather jackets and motorbikes had no appeal. I was a Mod. By this time groups like The Small Faces, led by Steve Marriott who sadly died in a fire when still young, and The Who exploded on the scene. New groups arrived on what seemed like an almost daily basis and they were available to their fans as live acts.

I wanted to break free and enjoy this new wave of music and expression. I hated school anyway. So when I was fifteen and the first opportunity to leave and earn some money arose, I left school. My cousin Barry helped me become a junior (*very* junior) Barrister's Clerk in chambers at 1, Paper Buildings in the Temple, London. The train journey to work from Northolt was long and arduous and the Circle Line on the London Underground was as bad then as it has always been, but I enjoyed the freedom my wages afforded me.

One of my tasks in Chambers was to go to the list offices at the High Court and at the Old Bailey. My boss and Senior Clerk, Arthur, would await my return before we checked the list of cases for the following day posted on a noticeboard in Middle Temple Lane. I was paid the princely sum of £5 per week. I gave my mother something for my keep, paid my fares, saved and still had enough left over to spend.

Even in 1963 that was a modest salary but we received very generous bonuses twice a year which virtually trebled the wages. The role of clerk was a subservient one and the counsels we served were from a very different class to my own. However, these men (and they were all men back then) were always respectful and polite.

On my sixteenth birthday I got a provisional driving licence and bought a second-hand motor scooter, a Lambretta LI 150. It needed a complete overhaul to make it a fashion statement but at least I had my scooter, a must for any aspiring Mod. I bought it from a dealership on the Uxbridge Road in Acton, West London.

"You ever ridden a scooter?" the salesman asked me.

"Course!" I told him but it was a complete lie. The minor detail of needing to practise had not entered my head.

I completely understood the principles of riding a scooter. The clutch was a lever on the left-hand side of the handlebars, the gearshift was a twist on that same side, the accelerator with front brake was on the other side and the footbrake was on the floor of the scooter. What could be difficult about that?

After a couple of jerky practice runs in the car park at the back of the shop, I set off for home. As I attempted to cross the busy High Street, I accelerated, slipped the clutch and raced across the crowded road, missing two cars by inches before hitting the kerb and flying off across the pavement into the bus queue.

The shop owner and dozens of passers-by rushed over to help me but only my pride was hurt. After dusting myself off, I had a few more practice starts off-road before very gingerly resuming my journey home.

Over the next few months I transformed my scooter. I spent every spare penny on it. I spray-painted it red, had the side panels, mudguard and front fairing chromed, added chrome carriers to the front and back, fixed a long aerial mast to the rear and topped it off with a fox tail. A 'Conti' silencer gave the engine a fruity, crackling sound to the exhaust. It probably slowed the scooter down but being a Mod was all about image, not the speed of our vehicles. We left that to the 'Greasers', our derogatory term for Rockers.

I lived for music, clothes and clubbing. Sport had been replaced and we went clubbing five or six times a week, always to see live bands. It might be The Who on a Friday, The Small Faces on Saturday and Georgie Fame and the Blue Flames on Sunday. My generation was blessed. It was possible to see and hear your heroes on almost a daily basis, at affordable prices. They were also accessible. I loved The Kinks who often played the Starlight Ballroom in Sudbury. In the pub next to the gig we bought whisky and cokes for Ray's brother, Dave Davies, before a roadie would come in and tell him his brother wanted him to go and get ready for the performance.

On leaving the Fender Club in Kenton during an interval before the main band, I bumped into a young guy in a white denim jean suit swigging vodka straight from the bottle.

"Hi Keith, what time you on?" I asked Keith Moon from The Who.

"When I've finished this," he said gesturing with the bottle as if to say have a slug.

Gratefully grabbing the chance to share a swig from Keith Moon's vodka bottle, I gulped down a mouthful and in a failed attempt at being cool I stammered, "Have a good gig!"

There were literally dozens of venues on the club scene. Burton's in Uxbridge was a club above Burton's clothes shop and it was popular with bands like Brian Poole and the Tremeloes and the Searchers. There were venues at the Southall Community Centre, the Blue Moon Club at Hayes Football Club where I saw people like Chris Farlowe and the Thunderbirds, Long John Baldry and Blues legends, Sonny Terry and Brownie McGhee. And there was a chain of clubs which included the Flamingo in London's Wardour Street, the aforementioned Fender in Kenton, the Crawdaddy in Richmond and the Rikki Tik in Windsor. We had live entertainment seven nights a week.

The Rikki Tik was an old rundown mansion on the site of what's now the swimming pool under the M4 spur road in Windsor and it was one of my regular haunts. Bands like Georgie Fame & the Blue Flames, Gino Washington and the Ram Jam Band and The Who would play until midnight, when the DJ would take over and spin records until four or five a.m. The venue didn't have a drinks licence so we'd have several before arriving. Those of us like me who were very tall could get away with looking eighteen and we bought for the rest of our friends.

We were young but even we needed a bit of help sometimes. Purple hearts could be purchased almost anywhere. A friend, Colin, had a dealer known as 'The Weasel'. He'd set up shop in the White Hart Pub Hotel car park in Southall where we could buy uppers, downers and hash ahead of the evening.

I didn't always take purple hearts as I always had bags of energy. I thought nothing of playing football twice on a Saturday, going on to party all night and then playing football on a Sunday morning.

Dating girls was an obsession for all the red-blooded lads in my peer group. My friend Andrew was very promiscuous and by all accounts lost his virginity by the age of fourteen. I wondered at the time what it was like for the poor girl who had her innocence taken away.

I had my first date when I was fifteen. I'd been made a Prefect and Head Boy. The teachers seemed to think I was mature for my years. Gillian was the Head Girl and word reached me that she fancied me. I walked her home a couple of times but think she tired of me asking her about her clothes and make-up. Conveniently for both of us, my leaving school and joining the ranks of the employed brought an end to our romance.

Meeting girls in clubs was easy for me. My distinctive motor scooter set me apart and I wore the latest fashions. It was clear that girls found me attractive even though I knew I wasn't particularly handsome and I hated the way I looked. A date for me usually meant taking a girl to a club where we'd dance. I'd buy her a drink, take her home on the back of my scooter and we'd kiss on the doorstep. Having sex with them held no attraction for me. I was attracted to them as mates.

Girls told me I was different and how they liked the way I took an interest in their clothes and makeup. As soon as we'd dated three or four times, I'd get scared and end the relationship. I must have seemed an arrogant young kid in clubs. I never shirked the challenge of asking a girl for a dance for a bet if my friends thought a girl was inaccessible and that she'd turn me down.

My friends thought I was something of a stud. What they didn't know was that it wasn't always me who ended the relationship. While many girls were attracted to my feminine energy, they only liked it if I could also be macho and be a man when it was needed. Here I fell short of their expectations.

After one particular night clubbing in London, I ended up in a flat with two friends and the girls we'd hooked up with. The other two couples were soon heading to the bedroom while I stayed chatting to the girl I'd met.

Becoming irritated, she asked, "Don't you fancy me?"

"Of course I do," I assured her.

"Bit slow, aren't you?"

Worried that I'd be exposed as a fraud, I started to leave before turning on my heel with a swift, "Actually, you're not my type," before slamming the door.

I didn't really feel that sex was something I wanted to do with girls, although I definitely didn't want it with boys. Sex was something I avoided but I also wanted to do it to prove to myself I was 'normal'. I had several attempts but never ever managed it. I became frustrated and avoided situations when the opportunity was likely to present itself.

By the time I was seventeen, working as a Barrister's Clerk had lost its appeal. "Yes sir, no sir, I'll make you tea, sir" had begun to irritate me and the class difference had become a source of annoyance. I was looking for something different.

One of my friends, Stephen, was working at Ladbrokes, the bookmakers. Stephen was horse racing mad and developed a serious gambling addiction. He told me I could get a job earning £17 per week (by then I was on just £7 as a Barrister's Clerk) and there was loads of overtime. Better still, the office was just off Carnaby Street which by now, along with the Kings Road, was the Mecca of the fashion world.

Game over. I could earn enough money to buy all the clothes I wanted and I could go clubbing seven nights a week. I gave a week's notice and began life as a Poster/Offsetter with Ladbrokes. In the days before computerisation we entered every pink betting slip by hand into a manual. We also had to place the white copy in front of a large machine card and offset it from the edge of the card so that the machine operator could easily see it and enter it into the machine which stored the account information.

I was amazed by the sums of money being placed by the clients. Lord Whoever would have £1,000 each way (£2,000 bet) on a horse at a time when the average wage per annum was less than half that amount. My Socialist principles were certainly not hindered by the experience of working at Ladbrokes.

Approximately twenty of us did this brain-numbing job day after day. When the Derby or the other Classics took place, the volume of work quadrupled and we could work any amount of overtime. I'd spend the Saturday night in a club such as The Last Chance in Soho, go for breakfast at throwing out time around five or six and then clock on for a ten-hour stint at work.

I remember buying a blue suede coat from Lord John in Carnaby Street to discover that it cost more than my dad earned in a week. He was angry and, looking back, he was probably a little ashamed by the fact that at the age of seventeen I was spending more on a coat than he could earn.

Drugs aside, by the time I reached eighteen, the legal age for drinking, I was already a very experienced drinker. Along with my friends I'd down five or six pints in a session and top it off with a couple of gins or vodkas.

We were indestructible, or so we thought. Looking back, those days were some of the happiest of my life. I had no responsibility, money in my pocket and the freedom to go out seven nights a week. I could fill my time with clubbing and drink myself into oblivion to put any questions about my gender out of my mind. I could also buy whatever clothes I wanted. By the time I was nineteen, after a four-year period of abstinence, I was again buying women's clothes to satisfy my need to cross-dress.

Although they were cheap and of a basic quality, C&A was the easiest place to buy girls' clothes. The store had a system where I could exchange a garment within a week and get a full cash refund. I'd buy a garment 'for my girlfriend', wear it a few times behind locked doors at home when I was on my own and then return it within a week. I rotated the stores, which was easy to do because there were three on Oxford Street within walking distance of work.

I avoided any likelihood of arousing suspicion that they were for me by also going to Kensington and Chelsea. I felt such shame over my desire to look like and be a woman that I'd go to any length to hide my 'dark secret'.

Although the job at Ladbrokes was well paid, it wasn't a positive career move. It was a dead-end job really, but it was full of interesting characters who, like me, were marking time whilst deciding what to do with their lives.

An Irish lad named Richard became a friend. He was a highly intelligent University graduate who invited me to go to Dublin for a holiday, which I did in the winter of 1967. I took my very first flight on an Aer Lingus Viscount, a prop jet. It was a cheap 'Star Flight' as they were then named which took off at about 22.00 hours. I was thrilled but a bit nervous of flying in the dark. My nerves were not aided by the neighbouring passenger, an Irish priest who downed several Irish whiskeys and counted his rosary throughout the short flight.

I enjoyed my stay in Blackrock just outside Dublin. Richard was a great host and took me into the snow-covered hills and mountains. We went to the famous Abbey Tavern and drank copious amounts of the famous black nectar. My love of travel had been further fuelled. I loved Ireland and found the people friendly and courteous.

Another intelligent misfit at Ladbrokes was an Australian named Aitor. The name is Basque and was passed down by his descendants who fought in the Spanish Civil War. Aitor was working his way around Europe. He'd invite derision from the boys and girls in the Ladbrokes Poster/Offsetter department by owning that he was a Beethoven fan. He was also a complete 'petrolhead' who was fanatical about Ferraris and motorsports.

Aitor and I had a similar sense of humour and both loved *Rowan & Martin's Laugh In*, a cult American TV show that launched Goldie Hawn. Her character was an archetypal dumb blonde which, of course, was far removed from the actress herself. Women like Goldie and Meryl Streep broke ground and successfully fought the male-dominated system to afford opportunities to generations of women who aspired to break into the world of TV and the Arts. They were real trailblazers.

Aitor loved sports car racing and had harboured an ambition to see the Le Mans 24 Hours race. Student riots in Paris during 1968 meant the race was moved from June to September. Aitor asked if I'd like to go with him on a coach trip run by a tour operator. I wasn't particularly interested in the cars, but it was France. The imaginary smell of a freshly baked baguette and the image of a glass of claret was all I needed.

We set off and survived a very rough passage from Southampton to Le Havre. On arrival in the French port we lost the coach driver until he was found in the men's toilets clinging to the toilet with his head hanging over the bowl. When asked what he was doing, he replied, "Praying this f*****g boat will sink."

Although I didn't share Aitor's love of cars, I loved the spectacle of Le Mans. Unlike Formula 1 which in my opinion is a boring procession, sports cars have different classes and engine sizes which means the cars can actually overtake each other. That was far more interesting than a sport where drivers follow team orders and either refrain from overtaking or hold back so a teammate with a better chance of winning the championship title can pass.

Visits to Ireland and France, coupled with a growing sense of needing to sort myself out with a career, had made me restless at Ladbrokes. The tedium of the work, the endless nights out clubbing and my ongoing struggle with my gender identity were all becoming routine. A visit abroad was destined to change my life.

In the summer of 1967 and into 1968, my social life consisted of clubbing, drinking, smoking anything and everything, dating girls and cross-dressing in secret. By the age of twenty I was becoming even more frustrated by the fact that whatever I did, the need to cross-dress wouldn't go away. It was always the same; applying makeup, wearing a dress or top and skirt and then wondering why I'd done it, taking it all off and weeping with the frustration and disgust of it all. My shame was so great, I'd go to the library where I read books about men who'd become women but I'd never check them out and take them away to read. That would have been too embarrassing. I'd read a chapter and replace the book on the shelf ready to read the following chapter the next day.

IMAGINARY CONVERSATION WITH OPRAH WINFREY

"Between stimulus and response there is a space.
In that space is our power to choose our response. In our response
lies our growth and our freedom."
Viktor E. Frankl

As any psychotherapist or psychologist will tell you, our early years shape the rest of our lives and it's the relationships with our parents that form the clay that moulds us and helps develop our character traits, both good and bad. These are also the relationships that provide the experiences that form our neuroses. In order to reflect on what I learned from my childhood experiences I decided to ask a hero of mine who'd overcome difficult beginnings to grow into a highly successful human being with great compassion for others. I had an imaginary conversation with Oprah Winfrey and asked her what she knew about growing, being seen and shining a light on others.

We have very different life experiences but I have a hunch that you know something about feeling different. I hated my body but you didn't have that experience. What was it like for a black girl growing up in the South? By the way, you were amazing in The Color Purple. *It was as though you had a real feel for the character and her situation.*

Slow down, that was two questions in one!! I think I'm getting an insight into you and your process. You try and do lots of things at once. Look, I'm not going anywhere! I didn't hate my body but I know what it's like to mentally split myself off from my body.

I think I know what you mean but please explain.

When people suffer pain or a violation of their bodies, they mentally 'split off' as though their bodies are somehow separate. That way they cope with the pain.

How did that come about?

When I was six, I moved to Milwaukee with my mother. I wasn't a desperately unhappy child but when I was a little older, I was abused by a relative and I ran away. They sent me to a juvenile home but fate took charge because they'd run out of beds and couldn't keep me. As a last resort I was sent to Nashville to live with my father.

How was that?

Well, he was strict but I always felt he wanted the best for me. Getting back to your question, I felt loved but I felt that nobody really understood me. How about you?

Nobody really knew who I was. I lived in a secret world because I knew who I was but was totally unacceptable to the people around me. I felt nothing but shame because I felt like a freak. I found a way of splitting off. What I mean is that I imagined that I was somehow separate from my body. It was as though my life was a movie and I was an observer rather than participating. It was my way of coping. How did you cope with what happened to you?

Well, I did what I guess you must have done. Aside from splitting off, I just took one day at a time. Sometimes we don't understand what's happening or why but we have to just dig deep and get through it.

What I find interesting about you and what connects with me is that despite all your experiences you truly love people and you are genuinely interested in them. Why do you think that is?

Well, I always have been. Perhaps it stems from trying to make sense of my own life and what was going on. I think it gave me an insight into human behaviour.

You have a lovely, grounded empathy, an ability to put people at ease.

Well, don't you? You work as a psychotherapist so you must do that too.

I do believe that working through my own issues has given me the ability to work with people experiencing theirs.

If you survive difficult experiences: you can either deflect from the memory by trying to erase it, or replace it with new experiences. And you can become inquisitive and seek out a deeper meaning. When we look deep inside ourselves, we understand that everyone has their traumas and their challenges. I don't think there's a person on this earth who hasn't had life-changing experiences.

We may not see it at the time but we know that those of us in the West are very privileged and we have opportunities that some people will never get. But our personal journeys are just that, personal to us and they're very challenging, often very frightening to us. I don't believe there's a league table of pain and I think the expression 'there's always someone worse off than us' can be damaging because it implies we should simply get over it, whatever the 'it' is. Whatever your experience, being alone at night in a dark room can be scary.

For me that part was terrifying. I used to think I was the only one, that my fear was unique and maybe it was my fault that my brain and body didn't fit together.

As children, we do sometimes feel trapped but when we become adults we find we have choices and we have to find the courage to make those choices and live with them.

Another thing I love about you is the fact that you had very little going for you and yet here you are, one of the most successful women on the planet. More than that, you're an inspiration to the people you meet. I felt as though I was banging away forever trying to find my purpose, yet you got to be where you are when you were much younger than me.

Yes, but does it matter? I mean it's where you are now that counts. Where you were yesterday is history and where you'll be tomorrow is pure supposition. We're only alive now!! I believe we have to make mistakes to find out who we are not before we know who we are.

That's easy to say but it can be tough, can't it? I was always striving for something. Did you have a sense of searching?

Yes, I did and you know what — that never stops. Maybe, just maybe, it's that journey that's the real purpose. Imagine what a waste it would be if you'd lived a dull, comfortable existence and never had any pain. If you had no pain you wouldn't know the joy of love. Would you have found out who you really are? I don't think so. You take the action and the insight follows. You don't think your way into being yourself. We're all too afraid of failing. If we could only stop fearing failure and understand that we have to find out what doesn't work in order to find out what does.

I always loved being on stage even if the stage was the back garden or yard. What was your first memory of being on stage and what was it that made you want to be an interviewer?

I've always been fascinated by people and interested in what makes them tick. I'm fascinated by people's stories and what they have to teach us. You know, growing isn't something that stops when we reach adulthood. Our bodies may stop growing and although they start ageing, our minds carry on growing and never stop as long as we feed them with the right nourishment. Why, oh why are we surprised when a kid uses violence when he or she is fed a daily diet of it on our television screens?

If I've done well, I think it's because I genuinely love what I do.

I've always admired you because you seem so real, so authentic. I think that's been my greatest challenge. It took me sixty years to become real. When I was growing up, I was fearful that the world would hate me if it really knew me. I had a crippling fear of rejection.

But that was your lesson when you were growing. You wouldn't be who you are today if you hadn't lived and worked through that.

True! What's the big lesson for you when you reflect on growing and finding your destiny?

The most important thing is to understand that we often don't realise who we're meant to be because we're too busy trying to live out someone else's ideas. Because we feel insecure, we let other people's opinions influence us and define our own destiny.

In my case I believe God told me to seek a higher path. I was trying to do what everyone else did and impress them but then I realised that when we shine a light on others and cause them to shine, we feel so much better about ourselves. When we feel better about ourselves, we shine our own light and the circle is complete.

4
MY FIRST ODYSSEY

"The world is a book, and those who do not travel read only a page."
Saint Augustine

—◦○◦—

I gave up smoking for a year which meant I ate like a pig and put on two stones or thirty-odd pounds in weight. Endless fried egg sandwiches from the cafe opposite Ladbrokes, when we worked late, and fry-ups at lunchtime at another café around the corner didn't help. My average daily intake of about six pints of beer probably didn't make a positive contribution either!

So, I'd gone from skinny child to slim teenager, to bloated and overweight twenty-something. I felt crap. My clothes from C&A had gone from size 12 to size 16. I resolved never to need a size 18, started smoking again and lost the weight within a few months. I became restless and was feeling lost.

I hung out with a group of guys from my old school in those days. There was Harry, a great guy who only ever wanted to listen to Bob Dylan, love someone and be loved; Dave the clown of the group; and my old friend Andrew, the gymnast who'd seemingly lost his virginity almost before he could walk.

When I wanted to hit the club scene, I hung out with another Dave and his 'team', as they were known, from Slough. Dave was the little kid who cried on his first day at school when another boy took his toy plane. Brought up on the Britwell estate in Slough, Dave had developed into a streetwise lad who could handle himself. He also rivalled Andrew in his ability to attract the opposite sex.

The guys in Slough would go out drinking on a Friday night, then go on to a club to begin the weekend. It was fun but there was always an undercurrent of violence. If the mood took them and just for a bit of fun, they'd target a bouncer at a club like the Top Rank ballroom in Watford and start a fight. A drink spilt or a wrong word in the wrong place and it would all kick off. I always sensed it coming and would quietly slip away. I may not have been much of a lover ... but I certainly wasn't a fighter.

Although Andrew loved music, he loved getting laid more than anything else, and he didn't struggle to find willing partners. But in 1968 the lover appeared to have been tamed when he got engaged to a slim Indian girl called Olga. I think he loved her but it wasn't long before he began to feel trapped and unsure about his future. One day, over several pints in our local, The Load of Hay pub in Northolt, the subject of hitchhiking came up.

Andrew liked the romantic notion of standing by the roadside with a harmonica in his hand while we waited for a sports car to pull up with a model at the wheel. This gorgeous blonde would invite us to take a ride, take off her clothes and make love in a haystack with him.

I was a little more conservative but the idea of travelling without a destination and an open road to anywhere fuelled my imagination. I'd read Laurie Lee's wonderfully romantic book *As I Walked Out One Summer Morning* and was captivated by it. His poetic musings on life on the road conjured up vivid pictures and had given me itchy feet. And perhaps I could leave my mental torment behind.

I can't remember who first suggested it but in the space of a few minutes, Andrew and I agreed to hitchhike to Greece and that we'd set off the following October. We reckoned we needed six months to save the amount of money we needed.

Work at Ladbrokes had tailed off and the overtime was drying up. The job was always boring and it had evolved into a tedious drudge so I spent as little time as possible at work. And anyway, things were changing at Ladbrokes. Computerisation was happening and the whole of the second floor was taken up with a new massive computer that probably had less power and less disk space than a 21st century mobile phone. Adapting to become a computer operator was not something that excited me. I hated the job to the point where I couldn't face going in. It was definitely time for a change.

Andrew said the local swimming baths paid good money for pool attendants so we decided to apply. The day I went to hand my notice in at Ladbrokes my boss called me to a meeting. His office was being decorated and so we met in the broom cupboard. It was hard to imagine less salubrious surroundings for my 'career' at Ladbrokes to draw to an end. I knew he wanted to demote me or sack me so my resignation was like a pre-emptive strike.

Everything has its time and its place. Carnaby Street was disappearing along with the swinging sixties and my teenage years. Brands like John Stephens had expanded and opened branches in the Kings Road and Oxford Street. A generation had had its revolution and moved on. It was time for me to move on too.

The swimming pool in Northolt was only intended as a six month job. Our intention was to do lots of overtime and then leave. During the interview I remember thinking, "Does this guy really think I'm serious about a long term career here?" but I played along with the pretence and got the job.

Just like Ladbrokes, the swimming pool was a dead end job but for us, it was bearable because we had an end date firmly fixed in our minds. Andrew and I were ready to leave for our adventure.

We bought rucksacks, sturdy hiking boots from the camping store and two train and ferry tickets to Amsterdam, where our journey would begin on the road to Athens. With £60 in my pocket and a guide called *Europe on 5 Dollars a Day*, I was finally free.

After a night in Amsterdam we set off for the autobahn. It took a couple of hours to thumb a lift to Arnhem near the German border.

We were beginning to realise that hitching across borders could be tricky and drivers were suspicious. We decided we'd have to walk to the border or maybe get a train across.

The day was hot, the walk was long and my shoes were new. Andrew was really suffering as it was his turn to carry the tent and he was wilting under the strain. The romance of hitchhiking was wearing off for him but with every step I took further away from England I was feeling more and more liberated.

With nightfall approaching we decided Arnhem was a step too far so we found a field just outside the town and set up camp for the night. Andrew unpacked a six-pack of Amstel from his rucksack. It was no wonder his back was breaking from the weight! We drank all the cans of warm beer and drifted off to sleep. It was the end of our first day on the road.

Daybreak was announced by a mooing cow as she nudged her nose through the tent opening. Five minutes later we were up and walking towards a farmhouse asking if we could buy breakfast. The friendly farmer and his wife invited us in and gave us a wonderful breakfast of ham, cheese and eggs washed down with delicious Dutch coffee. When we offered to pay, he smiled and said hospitality was his privilege. It was the first of many episodes of generosity we received whilst travelling. Luckily for me it's one of many, many similar experiences of human kindness I've had the good fortune to experience in my life.

We began to get the hang of this hitchhiking thing. There was no point trying to hitch across borders unless the driver knew you. It was too risky for them because they got into trouble if your papers weren't in order or, worse still, you were smuggling something. So, we bought rail tickets to Oberhausen, the beginning of the autobahn in Germany. From there we planned to head down to Austria and what was then called Yugoslavia en route to Athens.

After an hour's wait in the rain on an Autobahn slip road a small Renault slowed and then started to accelerate before again braking and reversing alongside us. In such moments lives change forever.

The passenger window wound down and a striking woman in her twenties with long red hair asked in an American accent,

"Where are you headed?"

"Athens," Andrew called back to her.

"But anywhere south will do," I added.

The driver was another American woman of similar age with long dark hair. She peered out at us.

"We'll take you south aways," she said in a New York accent.

The girls were cousins. Jean was from Boston and Ellen was the New Yorker. They'd picked up the car in Paris and were touring Europe. Jean was in between careers and Ellen just wanted to travel.

We talked about everything to do with our two countries, from the cost of a McDonald's franchise to the fact that British soldiers in Germany always appeared lost and were constantly seen poring over maps in their armoured vehicles. We tested each other on political views and to our relief we discovered that, like virtually all American youth then, they were deeply opposed to the war in Vietnam.

Jean's brother was a B52 pilot disaffected with the war. It was 1969, the year America finally realised they were in Vietnam under false pretences and were propping up a corrupt regime. It was the year they began to take action. Celebrities like Jane Fonda and her politician husband, Tom Hayden, were speaking out. It was no longer anti-American for people to take a stand against the war. 1969 was when every American knew a family with a boy who'd 'come home in a box'. That was the year when Woodstock raged against the Vietnam War.

The music was the glue that held it together as a protest vehicle and my, how it worked! Along with demonstrations on campuses across the US, Woodstock was the moment when the youth of America said to their government, "We will not be conned by your anti-communist rhetoric. This war must end." President Nixon couldn't get away with calling the students 'bums' any more.

Within three years the inglorious retreat from Saigon ended the war in 1972. Nixon took the dollar off the gold standard a year earlier in 1971 and the West has been printing money ever since. I believe this was the root cause of subsequent recessions and the so- called 'Credit Crunch' beginning in 2008.

That first night we stayed in a 'Pension' in Germany's Rhine Valley wine region. Over several beers and glasses of wine we put the world to rights and connected, retiring to our beds late into the night. I'd seen the look in his eye and I knew before Andrew told me that he fancied Jean. He was going to make a play for her the next day and asked me if I was okay about it, as though my answer would have made any difference.

All the next day there was an atmosphere. Jean and Andrew were spending time talking to each other but I wasn't making a play for Ellen. Andrew asked me to go for it for his sake, even if I didn't fancy her. The truth was I did like Ellen but I knew that being in bed with her would be a disaster.

We arrived in Munich, home to the Olympics in 1972. The city was dominated by the construction of the Olympic Stadium, the 'Spiders Web' as it became known in deference to the stadium roof which was a strange mesh affair.

My first night with Ellen was not too difficult. We were all exhausted and I had a 'headache'. The same thing happened on the second night. In the morning it got back to Andrew via Jean. He told me that unless I (literally) held up my end, the girls were going on without us. Andrew pleaded with me to get on with it.

When we got into bed the next night in Salzburg, Ellen told me she was a virgin and she wanted me to be the one to take her virginity from her. So, there she was thinking I was an experienced lover and I had no more experience than her. I was petrified.

Picture the scene; a guy and girl next door screwing like rabbits and two twenty-one-year old virgins in the next room. This time I tried, I really tried but I couldn't do it. I just couldn't make love. It all felt wrong to me, but I couldn't share my thoughts with Ellen.

We gave up. It was four o'clock in the morning. The pre-dawn quiet seemed to fill the room. The silence was deafening. She squeezed my hand.

'It doesn't matter," she whispered, like millions of women throughout history. I turned over and away from her in embarrassed shame. She draped her arm over me as if to say 'I haven't left'. I stared at the window, at the black night waiting for the dawn which didn't want to come. Eventually we both went to sleep.

I wasn't sure how long this could go on for but the next night in Vienna Ellen and I got very drunk and it happened. I was able to sustain the necessary lead in my pencil and we consummated our relationship. So much for alcohol being a passion killer. In my case it dissolved my inhibitions and took away the nerves. My immediate reaction was one of great relief. I thought I'd banished that female instinct that had been with me throughout my life forever. Now I was 'normal'!

We made love at least once a night during the next few days and all the way through Yugoslavia and into Greece. We were a couple and we were having a great time. It was as though I'd hypnotised myself into a temporary normality and I wanted to be hyper-masculine.

I was struck by another paradox at that time. While Strauss was being played everywhere in Salzburg, the home of Mozart, Mozart was being played all over Vienna, the home of Strauss. God knows why I remember that but perhaps it summed up the paradox within me.

Yugoslavia was a country of contrasting cultures. It was very industrial in the northern cities of Zagreb and Belgrade and very feudal down south in Sarajevo, Skopje and Srebrenica. Even then in the Sixties the inequalities that would later erupt into war were clear.

We agreed we'd all stay together for the rest of the trip, at least as far as the Greek islands which were our goal. We all loved Athens. Who wouldn't? It had everything. The Acropolis and the Parthenon, little tavernas serving Demestica wine and cheap yet good food. Over the usual glass or ten of wine and beer we decided to go to the Aegean island of Hydra. Why Hydra? I think we liked the shape of the island on the map!

Hydra lies just a couple of hours from Piraeus and it had no hotels and no roads. The island was barren, importing its water from the mainland. It was dominated by a small port with a crescent-shaped harbour bordered by tavernas. We took one of the narrow, winding paths leading up and away from the harbour to a taverna called 'Leto's' where we stayed for the equivalent of 20 pence or 30 cents a day.

To give it its full title, Leto's Place had a small restaurant serving squid, whatever other seafood was caught that day and the obligatory lamb. To entertain the girls Andrew and I would put a few drachmas in the juke box, get out a hanky, hold it between us and dance to *Zorba the Greek*. Every day we sat by the harbour and caught fish and squid, which we took to Leto's, where we ate it for free.

Hydra gave me time to empty my mind of all my worries and to really unwind. It was the first time that I'd ever felt really relaxed. The highlight of the day was the cannon firing from the small naval quarters on a rock overlooking the harbour. This was the era of the Greek colonels led by Papadopoulos and they liked to remind the locals who was boss.

Life carried on at this frantic pace for about six weeks. But our £60 was running out and we couldn't stay on Hydra forever. The island was home to many artists and writers but we decided we had to earn a living. We had to leave.

Now, I wonder why anyone *has* to leave a place like that. We all spend our lives building careers, working hard and stressing out. For what? So that we can retire to a small island and fish all day. What is wrong with us?

We headed back to Piraeus and took a ferry to Italy on the homeward leg of our journey. None of us really wanted to go and we delayed our departure at least three or four times before finally having a long liquid lunch and boarding. We had second class tickets (one up from deck class) on the *SS Kolokotronis* bound for Brindisi.

The *Kolokotronis* was a large ferry and it lacked the luxury you might expect on modern-day ships. It was in desperate need of a refit and a lick of paint. We had tiny cabins with barely enough room for two bunk beds. We set sail, bound for Patras, Corfu and Brindisi.

Whether it was the pungent smell of the diesel or something we ate, we all became ill with diarrhoea on the first night. The smell of diesel comes back to me as I reflect on the memory of frequent visits to the toilets which were awful, cramped dirty chambers. By the time we arrived in Brindisi, the idea of hitching was out of the window. Ellen and Jean took it in turns to drive and we made our way along the Adriatic coast to Bari.

On a road outside Bari we came across a small café. I walked in and in my best phrase book Italian I asked for "Quattro Cappuccini per favore." The lady behind the counter called back into the kitchen, "Four white coffees, Anne!"

It transpired that Julie and Anne ran a cafe in Southend, Essex, and their idea of a holiday was to swap with two Italian relatives from Bari who ran their cafe in exchange for Julie and Anne returning the favour. After Bari, we turned west and headed across Italy to Naples and then to Rome, the Eternal City.

I fell in love with Rome and began an affair that would last all my life. Paris may be elegant, New York exciting but Rome has a beauty uniquely its own. I think it's the mixture of decaying history from the greatest empire sitting alongside modern vibrancy that places it apart from any other place on earth. The tiny streets in the old city of Trastevere alongside modern department stores in the Via Veneto and superb restaurants everywhere deliver a fresh experience whenever I visit.

Among the ruins of the Coliseum and the Forum Andrew and I faced the reality of our financial position and reluctantly agreed to train it back to Amsterdam en route back home. A few days later we had a modest meal with the girls and left with virtually no money on the night train bound for Amsterdam. Andrew was downcast all the way because he was in love with Jean. I wasn't in love with Ellen but I'd come to really like her and I wanted to see her again. They agreed to meet us a few weeks later in England after taking their car back to France.

We had a miserable two days on the train with only enough money for a sandwich each. Our demeanour worsened and was further lowered by the constant interruptions at the borders. Immigration was followed by customs on one side of the border and the process would be repeated on the other side. Each border crossing required four inspections. Travelling from Italy to Switzerland to Germany to Holland made sleep virtually impossible.

We missed the connecting train and day boat which meant spending the day in Amsterdam before catching the train for the Hook Ferry later that evening. As we shared a sausage from the automat at Amsterdam Station, we reckoned we had enough money to watch a movie. After weeks on the road eating smaller and smaller meals, our stomachs had lowered their expectations of food, both in terms of quality and quantity. The truth is neither of us really wanted to go home and we'd have done anything to extend the journey by just a few hours.

Andrew knew he had to face his girlfriend, Olga, back home to end their relationship. I had no direction, no idea what I wanted as a career and I knew deep down that despite a sexual relationship with Ellen, the eternal battle with my gender identity would continue.

We boarded the train and then the ferry bound for Harwich. The next day, hungry and thirsty, we joined the train for Liverpool Street Station in London. Andrew asked the buffet attendant if they could give us some tap water only to be greeted with a curt, "We don't sell water." Paid for bottled water was virtually unknown in 1960s Britain. Welcome home!

My mother was delighted to see me. She had a map of Europe on the wall she'd marked with a blue pen to trace my route. I'd mailed regular postcards from the major cities on my adventure. After my first proper meal in three days I went to bed and fell into a deep sleep. When I awoke, I went into a deeper depression over my future. The adventure was over. I was faced with the 'what now?' question.

I'd left school at fifteen and had two jobs. I'd hated both and neither had provided enough worthwhile experience to use elsewhere. I didn't have a clue what to do next and I didn't much care. Having borrowed money from my parents, the next few days consisted of endless drinks in our local in Northolt, where we recounted our travellers' tales to our friends.

The day we were due to meet up again with Ellen and Jean, I awoke bursting with the need to express my feminine self. It'd been months since I'd last cross-dressed and my parents were away that particular Friday evening. I got my well-hidden suitcase down from the loft with my various paraphernalia of makeup and dresses. I told Andrew that I had a date I couldn't break and asked him to apologise to Ellen.

Andrew was understandably angry but what was I to do? Tell everyone I'd rather not meet this lovely American woman because I wanted to stay at home watching television wearing a ridiculous dress from C&A? Tell them all I was a pervert who wasn't really a man? I hated myself and I hated what and who I was. I drank the contents of a bottle of Gordon's Gin and collapsed into bed.

IMAGINARY CONVERSATION WITH SPIKE MILLIGAN

"Though we travel the world over to find the beautiful, we must carry it with us or we find it not."
Ralph Waldo Emerson

This phase of my life was not so much about travel but about me finding myself. To reflect on this search I turned to Spike Milligan, the first of my comedy heroes. Spike had many struggles, particularly with his mental health. I've always loved his humour but I've also been moved by his struggle with his demons. I once wrote to him to wish him well when he was in hospital having one of his mental health episodes. Several months later I received a letter signed by him thanking me for my interest and wishing me well. It remains one of my most treasured possessions. My next imaginary conversation is with Spike.

Travel's been a big part of my life, just like comedy. Your tales of being overseas must have been coloured by the fact you were there as a conscripted soldier. What did you learn from your travels?

I learned to keep my head down and that playing a musical instrument was a lot safer than firing a rifle. I didn't exactly *see* the world. Well, not unless being billeted in Bexhill-On-Sea in Sussex counts.

Apart from loving your comedy, I suppose I felt a connection when I discovered you were born in Lucknow, India, where my parents were married.

We're not siblings, are we?

Not unless my mother gave birth and shipped you off to Ireland, I don't think so! Growing up, you kept me sane. It's an odd thing to say to someone with a lifetime of mental health issues. Did you feel different?

Of course I did, but who the hell would want to be normal if it means being repressed and having to be polite to people you dislike and don't respect? I *was* different. I was Irish, I was from a country struggling to keep its identity. I suppose I always knew I wanted to do something on stage. In the early days it was music and jazz. So what's the problem with you being different?

I suppose for me it's all about how people perceive me and my shame in not complying with what everyone wanted me to be.

But that, my friend, is the biggest cause of stifled talent. Whether you are a writer, painter, actor, comic or anything else, you must let go of what critics think of you. I've had more people tell me they hated *The Goons* and *Q6* than I can count on the fingers of a thousand hands. They're all fools I tell you, fools! Listen, the army taught me that it's all bullshit. You have to be yourself and at least you'll always know that whether you do well or you fall flat on your face, at least you followed your own path in your own way.

That sounds almost spiritual. I thought you were an atheist?

Don't get smart with me. *I* do the funnies. If you like my humour, what was it you particularly connected with?

Oh, that's easy. I was always serious and your humour was just mad, insane, irrational, anarchic. You weren't trying to say anything other than 'come along and laugh with me,' and that's what I loved about you. Having said that, in your books you were both serious and funny. Was that intentional?

When I performed or wrote comedy, I just looked for the laughs. When I wrote my books, I wanted to tell a story as well as be funny.

Puckoon is the funniest book I've ever read. From the first line when you described falling off your bike right through to Ah Pong, the Chinese Policeman, it's a masterpiece.

Thank you, I'm glad you liked it. What I'm picking up from you is while *I* never gave a flying shit what anyone thought about me, you get wounded by people's opinions. Is that right?

I think it's more fundamental than that. I get scared and I assume they hate me and the pain of that will be unbearable.

Where does that come from?

Probably because I never felt that my father thought I was good enough and because I always felt like a freak, odd, different. No, that's not fair on my dad. He was distant but only because he didn't know how to connect.

Well, your father sounds like a man's man and you couldn't be the son he wanted. That's why you want to travel. You don't want to stay still because if you do, you'd have to be with yourself. You're a restless spirit. That's why you loved my work because I'm manic and I never stop moving. What my mental illness taught me is that you can't escape from yourself. You can't leave your problems behind by running away from them. All the life coaches and psychotherapists say you need to know where you want to be before you set off on your journey. But I have a different take on it. Most people don't know where they are *before* they set off. How can you chart a course if you don't know where you're starting from? I think before we make any major changes in our lives, before we start travelling, we need to know where we are. That's more important than knowing where we'll end up. In other words, it's not about the destination, it's about the journey.

I made changes in my life and I kept thinking, 'I'll do this when so and so happens or when this bit is right.' I never trusted I was good enough.

I used to bargain with God during the war even though I didn't believe in him. "Don't blow me up and I'll be good." We'll say anything when we're scared. Here's the thing though. We don't have to do this stuff alone.

I wish I'd asked God for more help. Since I've been here I realise I was taking the world on my shoulders and I should have asked for help.

For heaven's sake you don't have to do it on your own. We weren't called The Goon, there was an 's' on the end. Even Jesus had twelve disciples!!!

There you go again, you're not really an atheist!!

Smart arse! We can't make deals with God or the universe by running away and hoping all our problems will go away. I was treated appallingly by the BBC when they cancelled my programmes.

Fools, I tell you, fools they were. But art's about expressing yourself and comedy's subjective. I accepted people wouldn't like absolutely everything I ever did.

I'm not sure that's what I do. I think I'm too scared to stay still just in case I have to look in the mirror and see inside myself.

Well, I can understand what you're saying. I was a bit like that and I wrote comedy to take me outside of myself. Why don't you just do that? Just get on with life and see what happens. Just get on with it.

I've always loved performing but I know a lot of promoters think I'm too old or too something or other.

There you go again, worrying about criticism and other people's perceptions. Look, we all want to be loved but our insecurity, our fear that we're too much or not enough just gets in the way. Here's the lesson I learned; when we have a creative spirit, it can only flourish when you remove the fear. Fear blocks the energy because subconsciously we're censoring ourselves and our internal voice tells us, 'It won't work, they'll hate it.' Then we censor ourselves so well, we end up not writing anything or ever getting behind a microphone. Do you think we'd have created *The Goon Show* or *Q6* if we'd worried what people thought? Of course not!

How did you convince the commissioners at the TV companies?

In those days they weren't driven by fear. Now it's all about the viewing figures and the advertisers. They go for safety now, which is why there's nothing fresh or different on television. Some of it's good but a lot of it's rubbish. At least my rubbish, if it was rubbish, was *my* rubbish.

Spike, if you shared one lesson or had one piece of advice, what would it be?

Shoot the Pope, I tell you. No, I don't mean that. Well, only because it's murder. My lesson when bargaining with your Maker and the universe would be — don't chase success in the belief it'll make you feel fulfilled. Look at those deluded fools on reality shows. Seeking fame and fortune for its own sake is an illusion. Just go where your heart takes you. Free yourself to follow your dreams and then all the trappings of success (whatever success means for you) will be yours anyway. You are *different*. Why not embrace it as a gift rather than fearing it?

Your Maker?

OK, OK!

I knew you weren't really an atheist!

5
MARRIAGE

"When we married we didn't know very much. We were told the man is always on top. For years we slept in bunk beds."
Joan Rivers

———◦◦◦———

The world was my oyster. I was twenty-one years old with no responsibilities and no ties. There was only one small problem. I didn't know what to do with my life. I wasn't qualified for anything and had no obvious skills. I hated school and my teachers told me I wasn't clever so going back to study wasn't an option.

I knew what I *didn't* want to do. I didn't want a tedious repetitive job at somewhere like Ladbrokes and I didn't want to be a Barristers' Clerk. I was only interested in two things; clothes and travel. I had no obvious skills in either but I set out to explore the possibilities. The London Evening Standard ran an advert for a fashion house in the West End. I applied for the post of Delivery Driver which involved picking up garments from showrooms and delivering them to wholesalers.

At the interview a middle-aged guy with a large paunch and an atrocious comb-over of about eight strands of slicked down dyed black hair sat behind a cluttered desk in an even more cluttered office. He peered at me from behind his cheap looking cigar and eyed me up and down as if to say, "Why are you here?"

My conversation with him lasted all of five minutes. He stared at me through a cloud of pungent cigar smoke.

"Why do you think you'd be good at the job?"

I wanted to ask, "What is there to be good at?"

Instead I mumbled something about being interested in a career in fashion.

"You'll just be a van driver."

I had no answer to that. I hoped there might be some vague connection with my love of clothes and this very dull job. I left to the words, "We'll let you know," ringing in my ears, sure in the realisation that I didn't want the job and Mr 'Comb-over' certainly didn't want me. I never heard back from them. So, I'd even been rejected for the post of van driver. My humiliation was complete.

Since my only other passion was travel, I applied for a job as cabin crew to the then BEA (British European Airways) before it merged with the long haul arm, BOAC (British Overseas Airways Corporation), and morphed into British Airways. I got as far as the interview stage but I was turned down on the basis that I was too tall. They could have saved me a journey. I'd clearly stated my height on the application form.

Next I discovered a recruitment agency that specialised in travel agency staff and soon found myself being interviewed by the Director of Lep Travel in the City of London. Lep had a vacancy at their franchise store within Barkers of Kensington, a world famous department store. I'd be selling everything from package holidays to coach, theatre and airline tickets.

I got the job and turned up for my new post as Junior Travel Clerk on 1st December and met my new boss, Charlie. Charlie was in his mid-fifties, had worked in the States and had a false Atlantic twang of an accent. He introduced me to Bob, the Assistant Manager, Sue, a Senior Travel Clerk and a lovely lady called Betty who sold theatre tickets. She was an adorable woman in her sixties, plump yet elegant. She wore her hair in a curly bleached bob and her makeup was impeccable all the way to her bright red, shiny glossed lips.

Betty came from a theatrical family. Her father was a famous magician and her mother his glamorous assistant. Betty grew up travelling on the music hall circuit and from the age of five she became part of the act. Betty loved her connection with the theatre, even if it was only selling theatre tickets, which she did well and with childlike enthusiasm. Actors in between jobs or 'resting' as the euphemism goes, asked Betty when they wanted advice on what was worth seeing among the new crop of plays and musicals on the West End stage.

One of the benefits of my job was that I would occasionally get free tickets even if at short notice. I saw the premiere of 'Oh Calcutta' which caused a storm of outrage when it opened at The Roundhouse Theatre in London. It was the first play to exhibit full frontal nudity on the British stage and people like the self-appointed 'Tsar of Decency', Mary Whitehouse, seized on it as a symbol of the new decadence of immorality. Tony Booth, father of the former Prime Minister's wife Cherie Blair and star of *Till Death Us Do Part*, a ground-breaking sixties sitcom written by Johnny Speight, was the star.

It was a real privilege to see new plays on preview nights. I watched young actors like Tony Selby and Dennis Waterman in a Robin Maugham play *Enemy* before both actors went on to successful careers.

I loved the stage and watching these productions rekindled my enthusiasm for performing. I auditioned for a part-time course in the acting school at The Questors Theatre in Ealing. I got a place and had a grounding in the Stanislavsky method of acting. A very pompous voice tutor kindly informed me that unless I lost my London accent, I would only ever get roles like Michael Caine's. This didn't seem to be a very negative achievement and I ignored his advice. I was familiar with negative feedback from teachers but by this time I'd realised they weren't always right. It would still be many years later before I proved them wrong.

I got to know one of the customers while I was working for Lep Travel. Lady Cholmondeley-Brown was a stern, elderly dowager of a lady who looked like a character from an Oscar Wilde comedy. She had a box at the Royal Albert Hall and would let me use it when rock concerts were scheduled. This made me very popular with friends, who gratefully joined me for a free night out to watch the stars of the day, bands like Steppenwolf who recorded the soundtracks for the generation defining movie *Easy Rider*, Colosseum and Cream. When the lead singer of the American band, Mothers of Invention, Frank Zappa fell off the stage and broke his leg, the Royal Albert Hall called a halt to 'these unseemly Rock Concerts'.

Among Betty's many gay friends were a couple called Tony and Brian who were window dressers at Harrods. Tony often suggested I come to a party with them but I always politely declined. I was secretly confused about my gender identity but not about my sexuality.

Kensington was a fun place to be at the end of the Sixties. The legendary Biba was an iconic store and there was always a new shop or fashion store opening up. I became friends with some of the guys and girls running stalls in Kensington Market next door to Barkers. A bunch of us got together to have coffees or drinks in the local bars and cafes.

A charming guy called Freddie fascinated me. He was shy, had protruding teeth, long black hair and wore glamorous fur or Afghan coats. He was years ahead of the Glam Rock era personified by Marc Bolam and David Bowie. Freddie had amazing charisma. Despite his shyness he always caught the attention of the room the moment he walked in. Nobody who met him back then would have been surprised to learn he'd become a world-famous star one day with the rock band Queen before his tragic death. He had an indefinable star quality.

Around that same time I remember leaving work one day to see a newspaper billboard headline which read 'Jimmy Hendrix Found Dead'. I couldn't believe it. My friends and I had just seen him play at the packed out Isle of Wight festival after his seminal performance at Woodstock. It was a terrible tragedy. Then my favourite female artist, Janis Joplin, lost her life in a similarly tragic fashion. All my rock heroes were dying and all at the age of twenty-seven.

At least work was going well. My greatest asset was my encyclopaedic knowledge of geography. In this pre-computerisation era we worked out airfares by adding up the miles between predetermined routing points. In order to do this it really helped to know that Bombay was between London and Sydney or that Rome was en route to Cairo from London. Customers often asked for information or a fare to an obscure destination and they knew it would probably flummox the travel clerk. But I *knew* Pointe-à-Pitre was the capital of Guadeloupe and that Bamako was the capital of Mali. I soon became the 'go to' person in the agency whenever someone was stumped with a routing problem.

I'd barely begun my travel career when Christmas was upon us. Boxing Day was a working day and I remember being warned we might be busy. 'Busy' was an understatement. As I walked from High Street Kensington underground station along the High Street, I saw a lengthy queue snaking round the store and finishing at the side door next to the travel agency. Because this was the era of the package holiday, if you hadn't booked by New Year, you had very little chance of getting a holiday to anywhere on earth in July, August or September.

Up until this point overseas holidays were a preserve of the rich but when entrepreneurs like Vladimir Raitz founded Horizon Holidays and Tom Gullick founded Clarksons Holidays, it ushered in a new era of affordable holidays. By modern standards booking procedures were primitive. We literally had to phone over the reservation, get a booking reference and then post the application form with a cheque for the deposit to the tour operator. The most popular destinations were the Spanish resorts of Benidorm and Majorca but cheap flights were now available to most Mediterranean countries. Low cost flights to the USA and other long haul destinations were still a thing of the future in 1969.

My new employers generously allowed me to have three months unpaid leave and I flew out for a holiday with Ellen and her family in Connecticut. The town of Stamford, Connecticut was not the busy commercial centre it is in the 21st century but it was nevertheless a growing town. Ellen's family lived outside the town centre in a beautiful New England home built of brick and yellow beech timber, with an external chimney stack seemingly glued to the side of the house.

Ellen's mother was very welcoming but her sister had heard the story about me having a date with another woman on the day that Ellen and Jean were expecting to meet me back home in Northolt. I denied it but how could I tell her that really I was at home wearing a dress and drinking a bottle of spirits? She didn't believe my denial. Ellen and I still got on very well but a distance had inevitably grown between us. We were still friends, but the spark had gone.

During my visit I did the big American tour. I went to New York, Washington and San Francisco. In Los Angeles I stayed with a friend of a friend whose boyfriend was a draft dodger from the Vietnam War. I enthusiastically joined the group of dropouts and smoked grass incessantly. I spent weeks in a stoned haze.

Grass was so cheap then. We'd drive to a small town near the Mexican border and buy bagfuls for a few dollars. I think it cost less than conventional tobacco. The guys dodging the draft were always on edge, worried the Military Police might come for them any moment. Young men went to great lengths to avoid being called up or 'drafted' into the armed forces. A favourite technique was to stay up for three nights without sleep, drinking copious amounts of black coffee so they'd be shaking so much and their eyesight would be so wrecked, they'd fail the medical.

After about four weeks of self-indulgence I returned to the East coast to meet Ellen. It was an amicable meeting but we both knew our relationship was over. Founded on the excitement and romance of the road, we no longer had anything in common. And although I loved America, I didn't want to live there and she didn't want to live in England. We met briefly a few years later when I was on a business trip to New York. The last I heard, she'd married a successful TV executive and was living happily ever after in Manhattan.

I left Lep to join Preston Travel in Kingsway near Holborn, in London. We arranged trips for businessmen. There were very few women in senior business positions in the late sixties and early seventies. We were near Australia House in London so we were well placed to sell cut-price Jet-Ship tickets to Australia. £145 got you to Singapore where a Russian ship took you to Fremantle, all for one fixed price. This journey replaced the old postwar £10 assisted package to Australia for New World immigrants.

On one occasion a very flamboyant gentleman came in dressed in a black double- breasted coat with a large fur collar. He carried an ebony cane with a silver handle and his ensemble was topped off with a black Fedora. It was none other than Sir Noel Coward himself. I resisted the temptation to tell him how much I loved *Mad Dogs and Englishmen* as a child although I did mutter some sycophantic remarks about his acting.

He acknowledged me with a royal wave of the hand. He never spoke, preferring his companion to do all the talking while he regally distanced himself from the mundane conversation going on around him. I can't remember exactly what they came in for. I think they may have just wanted directions. It certainly wasn't for a £145 one-way ticket to Fremantle.

I enjoyed my work because I was in love with travelling. I was promoted rapidly and I became manager of a new travel agency in Harrow, a short bus ride from my home in Northolt.

Those few years from the age of seventeen to twenty-five were some of the most carefree and exciting of my life. With no real responsibility, I'd begun to see the world and my social life was one long round of drugs, booze and rock 'n' roll. Until Ellen, sex had been missing but I'd managed to put my gender dilemma out of my mind for much of the time. I'd accepted that cross-dressing would have to be my sordid little pastime. Aside from that I decided I'd be 'normal'.

Girls were great fun but I didn't want to marry one. I could be a great womaniser, date them and move on. But in 1972, that was all about to change. By the age of twenty-four my close friends had married and moved on. Andrew had married Jean and was living in America. Harry and Dave from Slough had also moved on. I became close to friends who were a couple of years younger than me. John was a sandy-haired guy obsessed with bedding women, something he appeared to do with ease. He had a degree in Physics from Brunel University and he serviced photocopiers for a living. Then there was Lenny who emptied gas meters. Lenny shared my love of music and clothes. He had a 'Rod Stewart' hairstyle topping his skinny frame.

The live act club scene had given way to the era of discotheque and nightclubs. The three of us loved clubbing. John inevitably ended up in bed with a woman, Lenny would go home to his girlfriend and I'd end up arranging to meet a girl for a date sometime in the future.

Glam Rock had replaced the Beatles and the Rolling Stones. Lenny loved Marc Bolam and I was fascinated by David Bowie. These guys were pushing all the gender boundaries out of the way. Rather than encouraging me, Bowie scared the living daylights out of me because I knew I didn't want to be a guy wearing makeup. But Bowie did confirm to me that I wouldn't be happy expressing myself with some form of gender variance as a compromise to actually being female.

A bug was eating away at me and it wouldn't leave me alone. My gender identity was distressing me and sex had again become impossible. I didn't want to make love with a woman as a man and I didn't want to have sex with men. I was literally in a no-man's-land. After Ellen I avoided sex for a couple of years until I once again tried to suppress my feelings and went out of my way to have sex as many times as I could. I thought it might help push the nagging feelings away but I always reverted to avoiding any kind of intimacy because it was too difficult and uncomfortable. I didn't want to fall for anyone.

The usual pattern was to pick up a girl in a club, try and get her into bed and then move on. If I drank enough, I could blank my mind off and sometimes sustain an erection for long enough to complete the act. But more often than not it ended in frustrating failure. Of course if I drank too much, I became totally incapable anyway and it was a convenient excuse.

I became moody and started drinking and smoking heavily. Being in the travel business meant duty-free booze and cigarettes were abundant. I was smoking about sixty-a-day-plus joints and drinking God knows how much alcohol. I became introverted and would go for days without socialising, preferring to stay in, feeling sorry for myself.

One particular Saturday in April 1972 I had decided to have one such weekend in, rather than going out clubbing or drinking. I watched a very depressing football match on television between England and West Germany, during which a blond German with large feet took England apart. Günter Netzer had reminded English football fans that the World Cup defeat of England in 1970 was no fluke and West Germany really was a superior footballing nation.

At the end of the match a friend called Terry knocked on the door to tell me everyone was going to a party in nearby Northwood and that

I should come. After watching Netzer humiliate us I was up for some light relief. Terry waited while I had a shower, dressed and jumped into his car en route to the Swan Pub in South Harrow, where we were meeting up with the rest of the clan.

John had brought a couple of girls along. I was very struck by one of them, a girl with dark curly hair and an amazing figure. She looked fun. Then I noticed her friend who offered me a share of her stool in the crowded pub. The friend was called Marie. It was the beginning of an enduring relationship, an extraordinary love story. It's a relationship that's survived more ups and downs than a theme park roller coaster.

Marie had a long layered blonde bob and was dressed in an extraordinary outfit with a red smock top under a trouser suit jacket, topping off large baggy trousers. The jacket and trousers were white and adorned with large blue and red bows. The trousers had massive 'bell bottoms' and the whole ensemble was by a fashion label named 'Miss Mouse'. I loved it. Marie's eye makeup was distinctive and right up-to-the-minute, pale blue and silver matte shadow, with long full lashes. I wasn't surprised to learn she was a fashion designer for a major fashion chain.

Marie and I talked and we kept talking. She gave me a lift to the party and I didn't stop talking for the whole journey. I tried to impress her by doing a selection of impersonations, which went down well. I was good at drinking and Marie matched me. She and her friend Gill dispatched a bottle of Scotch very quickly. The whole evening passed speedily. I wanted to see Marie again and when I asked her, for once I really meant it.

During a visit to see friends in Australia in 1972 I showed them a photograph of Marie and I told them she and I were getting married. This would have been news to Marie but I just knew it would happen. She was the first person I'd been able to talk to about almost anything and I wanted to spend more and more time with her.

One of the things I loved about Marie was her openness – she just accepted people for who they were. She had no problem with ethnicity, religion or people's beliefs. I was convinced that if we could love each other, I'd be able to push my feelings about being female away. I wasn't conscious of it at the time but deep down I hoped that if she knew my innermost secrets, she'd accept me and the action I might take one day. Sex wasn't particularly important to either of us although we managed to consummate our relationship. Making love didn't seem to be such a big problem because I really did love her.

In the autumn of 1973 after a holiday in Spain with her brother and his family, I asked Marie to marry me and she accepted. My parents were delighted. Marie's mother thought she could have done better but then she'd have said that even if Marie had taken the Prime Minister home.

Marie's father was already chronically ill when I first met him. Bill was a short grey-haired man with a fit and sturdy body. He was an ex-sailor and master builder but when I met him, his mind had become affected by pernicious anaemia. He had a major stroke while I was sitting at the dining room table with him in 1973. He never fully recovered and was detained in a mental hospital as it was then called in Hanwell, West London. To me it was still called the 'Hanwell Lunatic Asylum'. It was a horrible red brick Victorian building that looked more like a prison than a hospital.

It was like watching *One Flew over the Cuckoo's Nest* in real time. His mental and physical health deteriorated to the point where he didn't know his daughter any more. Martha almost stopped going there some time before his death. She believed they were breaking him down to make him more manageable and she couldn't bear to see it.

Marie and I set our wedding date for 21st September 1974. A family debate ensued. Would her father come from hospital in a wheelchair or not? But by this time his memory was destroyed and he knew little about what was going on. I agreed to go along with whatever Marie wanted but the decision was made for her when her father suddenly died from a heart attack. En route to the crematorium in Harefield we drove past the RAF base at Uxbridge and a young airman turned to face the road, stood bolt upright and saluted the passing funeral procession. It was a poignant moment.

Despite my resolve to banish my persistent desire to be female, it came back with a vengeance at the beginning of 1974, shortly after we'd set a wedding date. It was almost as though some great power had decided to attack me again and warn me not to go through with the wedding.

When I think of those times and later when the urge became uncontrollable, I'm amused that right-wing religious groups and so many people throughout society believe changing gender is an evil lifestyle choice. I'd have paid anything to find a cure and stop it.

In 1974 I didn't buy any female clothes but my mind was in torment. Sleep became difficult and I got depressed. I decided to seek a cure. I'd read that the Portman Clinic in London had a psychiatrist who specialised in curing people like me, people who were unhappy with their gender. Because of the fear of exposure I avoided my own doctor and opted for the private route. I can't remember what it cost me but any fee would have been worthwhile to end the torment.

My first brush with psychiatry was not a happy one. My psychiatrist was a bullish man with a thick neck and an even thicker Eastern European accent. He was an old-school analytical practitioner. I'd lie on the couch while he sat out of my vision at my head. Over several weeks he grilled me about my family and my upbringing during sessions of repetitive questioning. He appeared to be obsessed by the fact I had two sisters. Did they dress me up and encourage me to wear girl's clothes? Did I envy them? Did my parents favour them and make me jealous?

"Have you ever tried to cut your penis off?"

''Er, no," I replied. Whilst I hated it, even I knew that attacking it wouldn't magically turn it into a vagina, which was what I desperately wanted.

He nodded knowingly. "Ah, you clearly envy your Mother. You're not transsexual, you're a transvestite. We'll cure you."

He told me they could give me aversion therapy. I'd be hypnotised, take some nausea-inducing medication and if I wore women's clothing, I'd be sick. The idea was that I'd associate the wearing of women's clothes with the nausea and sickness. I was so desperate to find a cure I went along with it.

On one occasion I'd gone through this ritual at home, i.e. swallowed the pills, worn a dress and puked. I went out with friends to a club in the evening and had barely got inside the club when without warning I was sick, right there in the doorway. The doorman thought I was drunk and grabbed my arm and unceremoniously ushered me out into the night air.

I dreaded the medication. It was making me physically ill with the stress and dread of feeling physically sick. The worst aspect of this barbaric clinical treatment is that I felt constantly humiliated. The message I was giving myself was that being myself meant being sick. It meant I *was* sick. A sick pervert.

I was sick of being sick and stopped the treatment. Aversion therapy didn't work, and deep down I didn't want it to. Anyway, I now know I wasn't 'ill', it's just that at the time I would have done anything to feel 'normal'.

My last session with the psychiatrist ended abruptly. For the umpteenth time, he quizzed me about my relationship with my father.

"Do you get on with him?"

"He is a distant man," I said. "He was from a generation that doesn't express their emotions."

"Ah! So you hated your father!"

The irony wasn't lost on me. Only the night before I'd watched the aforementioned cult TV show, *Rowan & Martin's Laugh In*, where the Eastern European character had a running gag culminating in the line, "Very interesting, so you hate your father."

It was as if the past few weeks of emotion and tension had caught up with me in a single rush and I burst into hysterical laughter. My clinician was exasperated by my inability to stop laughing and my further inability to be cured. He threw his notebook down.

"If you are not taking this seriously, there is no point in continuing."

Still laughing I went downstairs, past the shocked receptionist and out into the balmy Hampstead air. I never went back and resolved yet again to try and put it all out of my mind.

Society's attitude towards transsexual people (the word 'transgender' had not been invented back then) was very negative in the seventies and I was prepared to do anything to find a cure. But you can't cure who you are. In 1974 I didn't like who I was.

My wedding with Marie was to take place at St Mary's Church in Northolt where coincidentally we'd both been christened. Marie was born in Northolt six months after me but we lived at opposite ends of the town and went to different schools. We must have brushed shoulders many times in the street but we never met until we were adults in 1972.

Everybody seemed to get married young in the seventies. My friend Lenny who was younger than me had married Barbara and I was one of the last to get married in my circle of friends. At the ripe old age of twenty-six, I was finally going to *settle down*. The 'Stud' had been tamed. Just how mind-bogglingly inappropriate that term was, only I knew. I reasoned that getting married and having regular sex would banish any crazy notions I still had about being a woman. Whilst I'd never managed to banish my constant craving to be female, I had largely controlled the urges to express my feminine self. I'd thrown away clothes and wigs many times but this time I told myself it would be permanent. I was ready to commit to being a husband.

We found a house in Holmer Green, Buckinghamshire which, in 1974, cost the staggering sum of £13,250. I worked around the clock to save my share of the deposit. All our friends thought we were mad when they learned of our 'huge' mortgage of £10,500. We were due to collect the keys the day after we returned from our honeymoon.

On the Wednesday before the wedding I awoke to an awful foreboding. I knew in my heart that my dark secret would never go away and one day I might have to face up to it. As the day wore on I became more and more distressed and I left work early. There was no way I could go through with this wedding. It wasn't fair on Marie.

I phoned her at work and asked if we could meet that evening.

We sat outside my home in my car in the dark. It was a warm evening but I felt cold as I gazed out onto the dark road ahead of me. There was a long silence as I struggled to find the words to speak.

"Marie, there's something you don't know about me. I don't think we should get married."

She turned her head and looked at me.

"If you knew what it was, you'd realise we could never be happy."

Marie shook her head and laughed a nervous laugh. "What are you talking about?"

"I … I just can't tell you." I heard a dog bark as though it was saying, "For God's sake tell her!"

She looked puzzled. "What is it? It can't be that bad."

She tried to get me to tell her but I couldn't do it. In the end she shrugged and gripped my arm.

"Look, as long as we love each other, whatever it is we can work it out."

And I did love her. By the end of an emotional evening we agreed to go ahead.

The 21st September introduced itself by absolutely chucking it down with torrential rain. But with only ninety minutes to spare before the ceremony it stopped and the sun shone. Our picture-book perfect day had arrived and the tiny chocolate-box church on the hill in Northolt was bathed in sunshine.

I showed up in my smart suit with wide lapels, baggy trousers with turn-ups and a kipper tie. Marie appeared in an amazing dress of oyster satin-crepe with batwing sleeves. She'd designed it, cut the pattern and made the dress herself. She finished it off with a swathe of delicately embroidered flowers. She wore satin pumps which she matched to the colour of the dress using tea to darken the fabric. It was one of the many techniques Marie had learned in the rag trade.

The reception turned into a great party which we left with reluctance at about eleven pm before going to the Sheraton at Heathrow. The next day we flew to Jersey for our honeymoon, a gift from my employer. When we arrived at the Sheraton, our double suite hadn't been reserved and the receptionist asked us if we minded a room with twin beds. After a row we got a double room but this mix up wasn't a great omen.

A week later we returned to pick up the keys to our new home. The departing owner had taken all the light bulbs and all the shops were closed. 24-hour supermarkets were a thing of the future. So, we began our married life together with a single light bulb borrowed from the neighbours, spending the first night in our new home in semi-darkness. It turned out to be an appropriate metaphor for the first few years of our marriage.

6
MY CAREER TAKES OFF

"For my part, I travel not to go anywhere, but to go. I travel for travel's sake. The great affair is to move."
Robert Louis Stevenson

My career in the travel industry moved forward quickly but in the mid-seventies a new genre of travel was emerging. Cheap flights meant a booming charter market, making it possible to buy seats in bulk at low rates. The quest for ever lower cheaper flights and travel brought about its first major casualty. The largest UK charter carrier collapsed and went into liquidation with the loss of thousands of jobs. The corporate world seized on the idea of offering tailor-made travel programmes to incentivise employees and customers. The concept was a winner and the market grew.

After our honeymoon Marie went back to work and I accepted a job from my old boss, Phillip, who was moving into this new branch of the corporate travel market. As well as chartering aircraft we had the contract to sell off cheap seats on scheduled services for Iberia and British Airways flights to Spain. It was hectic but great fun. We took our passports into work with us on a Friday. If there were any unsold seats, our partners came to meet us at Gatwick or Heathrow and we'd jet off to Malaga, Majorca or Madrid for a free weekend break.

The financial pressure of marriage and a mortgage sharpened my appetite for career advancement. I spent a year commuting two hours each way to and from work, suffering a twenty-minute car drive through traffic to Amersham station, an hour-long train ride from Amersham to Baker Street in London and a wait of up to twenty minutes before beginning a tortuous underground journey on the Circle Line to Gloucester Road. Enough was enough. I decided to make another career move.

I got a job twenty minutes' drive from home in Holmer Green. It was a drop in salary but I was exhausted from all the travelling. The owner of the travel company was a really nice guy but sadly his love of cricket and alcohol were not qualifications for running a business. After a year the company was taken over by one of the client companies and I was made redundant. I decided I'd never again place my future in the hands of an arrogant businessman who'd sack me without even finding out what I could offer.

But before I could achieve my goal I needed more experience. Within weeks I was working back in the West End with Periton Travel, a division of Grand Metropolitan Hotels. My boss, George, was a bullish man in his late fifties. Behind his gruff appearance he was a generous man who enjoyed a few pints at lunchtime but was good at his craft. He taught me a lot about chartering aircraft and negotiating discounts with hotels and overseas agents.

I soon got close to one of our biggest clients. The Watney Mann Truman Brewery (WMTB) Company was one of the largest breweries in the country and I developed the client into a massive revenue stream for our agency. The brewery in Brick Lane became my second office as I was so often meeting Marketing Directors to devise new incentive schemes for their clients. I discovered I had a flair for creating imaginative tailor-made travel programmes and I felt encouraged to start my own business.

We organised two-day trips to the Holsten Brewery in Hamburg for all the best clients. The visits were largely based around drinking copious amounts of Holsten Pils. This was followed by a tour of the city, stopping off at The Holsten Bierkeller on the infamous Reeperbahn for yet more alcohol. Here the organised part of the tour ended and the punters went off for an evening of drinking and strip clubs, with many of the men seeking out the nearest brothel.

For top clients we would add two nights in West Berlin which had become my favourite city. The city was an island surrounded by the infamous wall in East Germany. The Berlin Wall was a despicable symbol of the failure to agree on a sensible solution to the problem of administering postwar Germany. It seemed to ignite a 'live for the day' attitude with West Berliners which made it a really exciting place to be.

I could smell the history when we took clients around the city. We visited the East via Checkpoint Charlie by day and partied in the West at night. West Berlin was razed to the ground in 1945, and was consequently made up of modern buildings. Berlin has a grey image but it's actually a beautiful city with forests and lakes. In pre-unification Germany, West Berlin was a defiant symbol of the 'Free West'.

I always used the same tour guide for the sightseeing excursions. Heinz was a silver-haired Berliner with history etched on his craggy face. He was seventeen years old when Britain declared war on Germany. He survived the Russian Front, the Western Desert and was in the Berlin Garrison when the city was overrun in 1945. He had a complete grasp of the city's history and its sights. Heinz used to say of his experience of the War, "When you've seen the whites of your opponents' eyes, you don't talk about it."

But on one occasion over several glasses of beer and shots of Schnapps he told me how his life was saved by a malaria attack. During the battle for Berlin in 1945 he and four colleagues got cut off from their regiment and hid in an underground bunker. He was unconscious from the malaria when a Russian grenade was tossed in. One of the German soldiers was between him and the blast and unwittingly saved his life. The Russian soldiers mistook Heinz's malaria-induced coma for death and moved on.

He regained consciousness and under cover of darkness later that night crawled towards the West where he knew the Americans were. When he heard American voices, he surrendered. Going East would have meant certain death. Word had got round that the Russians weren't taking any prisoners. Heinz was twenty-three when the war ended. He was cleared of any war crimes and was later employed by a US General as a driver.

His experience made him the perfect guide. He mesmerised tourists with stories about hiding under Glienicke Bridge, one of the transit points between East and West Berlin as he witnessed the spy exchange of the U2 pilot, Gary Powers.

For me West Berlin really came alive at night. Travel literature is full of clichés: 'where East meets West', 'a unique mix of old and new' and 'the city that never sleeps'. But the one time these clichés were actually true was when they were applied to West Berlin.

The clubs and bars on the Kurfürstendamm were still humming with activity at 4 a.m. I discovered a more exotic side to the city after about 1 a.m. when I said goodnight to my clients on the pretext of retiring for the night and I went off to see Berlin's more intriguing night life.

There were clubs like the Kit Kat Club in the movie Cabaret if you knew where to find them. It was as though a corner of West Berlin was caught in a nineteen-thirties time warp. I chatted to transvestites and drag queens but I also met several transsexual girls who were working their way towards surgery. They saw me in my smart men's clothes and of course they didn't know what was going on in my head. They often dismissed me as one of the many 'tranny-chasing' punters in the club. Pre-operative transsexuals are in great demand by men who presumably can't easily own and be open about their sexual feelings and convince themselves they aren't really having sex with a man. Maybe it's intrigue or perhaps it's an attraction all of its own.

Berlin felt like my safe place where I rubbed shoulders with other like-minded souls who also didn't fit in with society's stereotypes. Here there was no 'normal' and I loved it. Lou Reed's *Walk on the Wild Side* could have been written for West Berlin. I loved West Berlin and West Berlin seemed to love me.

My client, the brewery company, as well as being licensed to sell Holsten also had the licence to sell Carlsberg Beer and I hit on the idea of chartering Concorde to Copenhagen as a one-off for their top clients. The trip proved so popular and so successful as an incentive prize we ended up running regular charters on a monthly basis.

We took off from Heathrow and flew up the corridor, a designated route over the North Sea, in order to fly supersonic. We went to Copenhagen for a fantastic lunch at the brewery before returning home. I'd become a valued client of many of the airlines including British Airways and they frequently gave me tickets to fly on Concorde to New York, Miami and Singapore.

Stargazers would have loved it. I sat next to the likes of Roger Moore, the then James Bond, Mick Hucknall and other rock stars as well as numerous politicians. Concorde was an amazing aircraft which nearly died at birth because the Americans initially banned it from New York because of the noise levels, before later granting it a licence. It was out of sheer jealousy in my view. Sure it was noisy, but what a great feat of British engineering!

There was barely a week when I didn't fly somewhere. I've been to every single country in Europe if you count the Soviet Union as one country. (All right, I know it's cheating!) My work took me to several countries in Africa, North and South America and most of the Far East. I loved my trips to Thailand, India, Hong Kong, Indonesia and in particular Malaysia, which I am especially fond of. I loved the modern vibrancy of Kuala Lumpur, the colours of the east coast region where batik and kite-making are a part of everyday life, the beauty of the Cameroon Highlands and the magnificence of the jungle in Sarawak on the island of Borneo.

The Malaysian tourist office wanted to put Borneo on the tourist map and arranged a familiarisation trip to Sarawak for me and five journalists. The journey started in a mini-bus in Kuching, Sarawak's capital. When we reached the river, we took only the clothes we wore and the plastic laundry bags from our hotel filled with a change of clothes and other essentials. We transferred to narrow boats that took four people including the boatman and we were rowed up river.

As we progressed we reached points where the river ended and we carried the boats for a few yards before returning them to the river, when it picked up again. These breaks became more frequent as the river gradually reduced to a trickle and the jungle became denser. After about five hours we reached a clearing and the Iban Indian village. These former headhunters were now pig farmers desperately clinging on to a way of life that was being threatened by the diminishing jungle.

We arrived with our Chinese guide and were met by the villagers and the Chief, an elderly man bronzed by the elements and stooped by the years. He looked about eighty but I believe he was younger. The hard life there had clearly taken its toll. His tattooed face was framed by his long earlobes, which were adorned with large brass earrings.

We stayed in a longhouse where I shared a floor with twenty or so families of Iban Indians. Longhouses are long wooden houses built on stilts about six or seven feet off the ground to cope with the daily rains. They were originally built to house several families as a means of defence if they were ever attacked.

With a toothless grin stretching from earlobe to earlobe the Chief presented me with a spear. The Chinese guide explained I was being offered friendship and I now had to spear a small pig which was squealing in a sack as it was held down on the steps up to the Longhouse. Tradition dictated we should then walk up the steps through the blood and enter their home.

The Dutch journalist quipped, "Don't waste a good pig. Kill the Kraut." It was a comment not well received by the German journalist who looked as though he wanted to spear the Dutchman. In the end the Frenchman rescued us all by doing the honours.

All the men in the village had extensively tattooed faces with brass earrings in earlobes which stretched to about six inches in length. I found it slightly disconcerting to see human skulls strung together in the rafters above the reed mat where I slept. On investigation, I discovered they were the remains of Japanese soldiers killed by one of the village elders in World War II. I was very polite to the elders in the longhouse!!

Lying in my luxury jungle accommodation that night I was unprepared for one of the most amazing experiences of my life. Waking up to the sound of the jungle is something that everyone should experience at least once in their lives. On my first night, having retired at nightfall, I awoke from a light sleep at around four a.m. It was the type of sleep when you don't quite know for sure whether you've slept at all. The crickets had ceased their chatter and even the nocturnal creatures seemed to have retired. It was the jungle that had woken me with its eerie silence.

Again I drifted into fitful slumber to be woken by a crowing cockerel followed by the cheep of a young bird announcing to the world he needed feeding. One by one the creatures of the jungle awoke to contribute to what quickly became a cacophony of noise. The New Zealand journalist and I were sharing a space in the longhouse. We couldn't hear each other speak, such was the intensity of the different sounds. I lay there feeling emotional as I pinched myself to see if I really was lucky enough to be there.

I've never ceased to enjoy the thrill of entering a new country. Every nation has a colour, a feel and an aroma of its own. It's as if the very flowers know they have an identity and know where the border is. Sometimes I've ached to visit a country and I've never been disappointed when I've gone there.

Always there are surprises. The wildlife of East Africa was every bit as sensational as I had imagined but I was blown away by the bird life with its vibrant crimson reds, emerald greens, deep blues and vivid yellows. Other times I'd not be looking forward to a visit only to find I loved the country and the people.

One such occasion was Jordan. I'd reluctantly gone on a trip after working too hard. I was feeling exhausted. My first surprise was to discover how friendly and hospitable my Jordanian hosts were. They were keen to befriend me and asked endless questions about life in England. I think they feel an affinity because we both have monarchies, although quite how that works I am not sure!

Bathing in the salty Dead Sea is a unique experience. On another trip I repeated the experience from the Israeli side. Swimming on both sides of the Dead Sea is a privilege denied to most people in that part of the world.

I organised a trek for sixty participants to cross the desert visiting old Roman forts. Next we drove over another hill to the very same steam train used in the film *Lawrence of Arabia*. We boarded it and chugged along the track back to Amman while Gypsy violinists serenaded the guests with the setting sun as a backdrop. Nineteen-eighties Jordan was very westernised. The Jordanian hotels arranged for waiters to serve champagne cocktails as the sun set in the desert.

My reputation and the reputation of the company grew as we became known as the 'go to' company if you wanted a creative programme. We were the people to seek out as we lived up to our name. We were certainly one of the top two or three in the country when it came to this specialist area of the travel industry.

I loved it all, but for me it wasn't work. Travelling to foreign lands, meeting new people and designing stunning travel programmes was simply a joy. Nothing could pay for the sheer pleasure of seeing the looks on the faces of people experiencing something unique.

Once I had a great budget for a trip to Bangkok and Bali. We held a theme party in the hotel grounds in Bangkok. We arranged for a Thai boxing match, amazing Chinese acrobats, the recreation of a Bangkok food market and a flower ceremony where lotus flowers and orchids with candles were floated out on the lake in the hotel grounds. The evening's proceedings culminated in a spectacular firework party. We had to get dispensation from the Palace in case the King thought a military coup was taking place!

The flight to Bali was eventful as the Garuda aircraft flew head on through a tropical storm. The turbulence was akin to being on a roller coaster. Halfway through the flight we were struck by lightning, hit an air pocket and dropped what felt like ten thousand feet. Several people were sick, one man broke his arm and a pregnant woman went into premature labour and later lost her baby. The flight should never have taken off and the airline was fined by IATA, the governing body, over the incident.

I pulled out all the stops to get the trip back on track which we did in spectacular fashion. My agent, Jimmy, and I put on an amazing theme party in the ruins of a temple. We made a cash donation to the local villagers who lit the place with torches and welcomed the guests. This was followed in the temple ruins by a Barong dance, a Balinese dance with face masks and beautiful costumes.

Women came up to me in tears from the emotion of an amazing evening, something they knew would never be repeated. Dozens of people said afterwards that the whole trip was the most extraordinary experience of their lives. For me this was job satisfaction at its best.

I picked up the language quickly in Bali and by my fifth or sixth visit to Indonesia I could enjoy a simple conversation with the local people.

If I was in the travel industry today, would I have done things differently? Probably. I think travel's had a negative effect on a lot of countries where skyscraper hotels have ruined beautiful landscapes and the barrier between the tourist and local people remains really stark. I hope a lot more thought goes into the development of tourist industries in the modern world, although every country will adopt its own approach.

In 1990 I was voted Chair of The Incentive Travel Trade Association and was at the very top of my game. But it wasn't long before outside forces and life-changing events challenged this position and I would soon be embarking on a very different journey.

CONVERSATION WITH GROUCHO MARX

"Before I speak, I have something important to say."
Groucho Marx

Laughter has been my saviour. Comedy and humour have always been a big part of my life and were instrumental in shaping me. Spike Milligan was my idol but the man who made me laugh more than anyone on the silver screen was Groucho Marx and his brothers.

There was the madcap humour of the silent Harpo, the banter with Groucho and his piano-playing brother Chico who was a genius on the keys but had a gambling problem. And, of course, the string of hapless women who were the butt of Groucho's legendary one-liners. Like Spike Milligan, Julius 'Groucho' Marx was not just a great performer, he was a brilliant writer and he'd probably jostle with Spike Milligan for top spot in any comedy writing genius awards.

What I find interesting and what really marks Groucho apart for me is the fact that whether in print, performing or appearing in public, he always wore a mask. He hid behind that greasepaint moustache and was always wisecracking, but it was often as a deflection. He was rarely, if ever, himself in the public eye. He was divorced three times and I reasoned he would be the perfect hero with whom to have a fantasy conversation about marriage and career. Some of the words are from Groucho's movie scores or quotes but all in a different context.

Groucho, my first question to you is about your heritage. Your ancestors, the Schönbergs, emigrated to the United States from Germany back in 1860. Did those roots influence you?

Talking of roots, yours need doing. There's too much grey for a woman your age. Stop looking your age and get to a hairdresser. Any self-respecting woman should get to the hairdressers every week. The world doesn't want to witness your ageing process. What was the question?

Your ancestors and their influence on you.

Oh yes. Well, of course they did. My ancestors were German-Jewish immigrants who needed to be very determined just to survive. That determination passed down to us. We grew up in an era where poverty was an everyday reality. I worked on stage as a kid with small audiences for no pay. That's why we worked hard and made a lot of movies. We knew how easily it could all disappear.

Were you fearful of losing everything?

No, we didn't let ourselves even think about that at the time. We just knew that doing what we loved had to be appreciated while it lasted because it could stop at any time. However hard we worked, we knew it was easier than working as a shoeshine. Talking of which, your shoes look dull. They could do with shining.

They're suede.

Don't be smart. Women should be seen and not nerds.

How did you get into show business?

It was in the blood. My grandfather was a travelling magician and my mother Minnie was in the act. Not *my* act, *his*. Why would I want my mother in *my* act? Are you crazy?

I didn't suggest it.

Good, I'm glad you agree. It would have been a bad idea.

I loved the travel business but I had to leave it. I've had other careers but I'm spending most of my time now on a platform, speaking and performing. I was never sure what my strengths were until I was much older. Were you always sure?

Listen. I lost all my money in the Wall Street Crash so I figured that wasn't for me. Some years later I actually went on the floor of the Stock Exchange and made a speech. I told them I figured I owned a part of it. In the end I just did what I loved. When you love doing something, you're naturally good at it. When did you ever hear anyone say I really hate my job but I'm really successful and have made millions doing it?

So, you loved what you did.

You tell me, how could I have run around with a bent back and a greasepaint moustache for years on end if I didn't love what I did?

What advice would you give someone struggling to find out who they really are?

Go find your birth certificate or ask your mother who she slept with. Better still, just think back to what you always enjoyed doing as a kid. Follow that question up with "What's the one thing I can do that most other people say they find difficult?" Lastly, ask yourself what you're doing for other people. If what you're doing has no benefit for others, you'll get nothing back in return. It's the Law of the Universe, but don't tell Chico. He thought gambling was specifically designed to put money in his pocket. He died owing me 10 bucks. What was my point? Ah, yes. Everyone runs around trying to be somebody they can never be because they don't believe they deserve it and they can claim they at least gave it a try. Whatever you have a gift for, get over yourself and do it. It's why you're here.

Wise words from a clown!

Who are you calling a clown?

You know I didn't mean it literally. How about marriage?

You're not my type. Well, I was married three times. I think marriage is a great institution. I just didn't want to be in an institution. Who said that first? Was it me? I had mostly happy marriages. Just because I was married three times doesn't mean I didn't like being married. I just got bored and so did my wives.

The women you played opposite on screen were long-suffering. How did they cope?

They didn't understand a word I was saying. In fact that's the secret of a successful marriage. Find a husband or wife who speaks a different language. Can you speak French?

You don't mean that.

What's wrong with French?

I meant you don't mean being on a different wavelength in marriage is a good thing.

You're right. Of course I don't. Marriage is the same as a career. If you love someone, you invest time in the relationship. We didn't get to be great performers by reading about performing. We learned by doing it. In a relationship we want to feel loved. We have to consciously do what we can to give and express love as well as just receiving.

You're quite the romantic. Is it as simple as that?

Well not quite. I got divorced more than once. It isn't simple at all. People change and we have to be able to adapt to that change. That's why people often drift apart. It has to be an equal proposition. If only one person in the relationship adapts, eventually they resent it. And anyway, the other person falls out of love with you because you're not the same person they fell in love with.

I think it's much healthier for people to divorce rather than stay in a marriage if it isn't a happy one. What's the point in denying the both of you the chance of finding love somewhere else?

Everyone wants love. Performers go on stage to get it, doctors and medics heal people to get it and crooks join the tax office to get it.

I read somewhere that, like the British comedian Peter Sellers, you were still wisecracking even in death. Is it true that your last request was to be buried on top of Marilyn Monroe?

That is an outrageous slur. It was my *second* last request. My last request was that someone paid my taxes.

So what advice would you give to someone making their way in life?

Just do it, do it, do it, keep on doing it. If you enjoy it, it'll work. A lot of people think work and making money needs to be hard. It doesn't. But that doesn't always mean success happens overnight. Persistence is everything, but you can't be persistent if you hate what you're doing. Now enough of the questions, let's talk about the weather.

The weather?

Whether you will or whether you won't?

One last thing, Groucho. I just wanted to tell you that in 1989, the Republic of Abkhazia in the former Soviet Georgia proclaimed Independence. To show the world they were rejecting their Communist past they issued two postage stamps. Instead of the revolutionary leader Vladimir Lenin, they used John Lennon and instead of Karl Marx they had your good self, Groucho Marx. I thought you'd have loved the gesture for its absurdity.

7

CHANGE AND ACCEPTANCE

"The ultimate lesson all of us have to learn is unconditional love, which includes not only others but ourselves as well."
Elisabeth Kubler-Ross

───────◦○◦───────

There are days in one's life that are imprinted on your memory forever. My second daughter's birthday was one such day and not only for her birth but for very different reasons to the usual experience of fatherhood.

My struggle with gender identity continued on throughout my life in waves. At times I put it to the back of my mind but it came back, crashing down on me and consuming every waking minute. On many occasions I wondered if *this* experience or *that* event might cure me and enable me to accept a body and a gender role I hated. From playing football to boxing, from sex to marriage and parenting children, nothing, but *nothing*, overcame the desire to be female.

When Marie and I discussed children, my head said it would be wrong but my heart reasoned that this at last might provide conclusive proof that I could make it as a man. It didn't happen when our first child Laura was born but perhaps it would happen when Susie arrived?

Susie's birth was another miracle. It was just as special as Laura's arrival. Marie went into labour in the late evening of 13th June 1983. Just as with Laura, after a fourteen-hour labour I held my daughter and cried tears of joy and amazement. After Marie and our baby were reunited I went home to share the news with parents and close friends, before picking Laura up from her nanny to come and meet her beautiful new sister.

When I arrived home I had an overwhelming desire to look in the mirror to see a female image. But it was the same old masculine image staring back at me. My home was silent for once. I heard a song thrush talking to the wind in the garden and my neighbour closing a car door before driving off to work. My heart was pounding in my chest. I broke down.

Something inside me snapped. I looked into the mirror and I choked out, "When will you accept that you are transsexual?"

I dissolved into floods of tears and pleaded with God and the universe. "Please, please take it away. Make the unbearable pain go away. Please cure me. I have a family to take care of."

Deep down, I knew I'd bargained with God for the last time. My life changed and there was no going back. Even if I didn't like it, I'd finally accepted who I was. Susie has been a great gift and her birth was liberating because I finally knew that even 'fathering' not one, but two children was not going to block out the woman inside me bursting to come alive.

Finding a way to accept yourself is the Holy Grail of the Self-Help sections of book shops everywhere. I'd never uttered the word 'transsexual' in the context of myself before but finally owning it brought me a sense of great relief. But that was almost instantly replaced with fear and trepidation over the enormity of what I was acknowledging. I'd stopped denying it but was still telling myself I could suppress it. I could wait until the children were adults and maybe share it with Marie when we were eighty-six years old. But right now in nineteen-eighty-three I'd acknowledge it, but I would do no more than that. I'd contain it. I was far too scared to do anything else.

I took Laura and Nanny to the hospital to meet a new sister and a great-granddaughter. Laura was dressed in a cute sailor suit and cuddled her new sister. A nurse walked past.

"Aah, look, I feel all broody," she cooed.

"You want to watch it, love. There's a lot of men on a short fuse in here," one of the several fathers in the maternity ward quipped. I remember laughing both at the amusing riposte and the absurdity of the comment when applied to me.

Major events in life never seem to arrive in isolation. There were also major changes going on in my career. David, my future business partner, and I were working for a large travel company before starting our new business venture. Our employer got wind of the fact we were starting a new business and were planning to take clients with us.

About a week after Susie's birth he called a meeting, challenged us and told us to clear out our desks. Our new business was born from the urgent need for an income. To some degree the enormity of my personal situation was put on the back burner. I just had to get on with it.

By September 1983 together with my new business partners David and Colin, who had been recommended as someone with a good business brain. We set up an office in High Wycombe, Buckinghamshire. The imbalance in our working relationship was apparent at the outset. David and I drove modest Vauxhall Cavaliers we'd taken from our previous employer as part of a tiny severance package. Since the cars were virtually worthless to them it was a good deal all round. But Colin bought a second-hand Jensen Interceptor. Having an absurd car like a Jensen on the company books was crazy. One of the guys from a business which shared the building playfully asked, "Is there a fuel tanker permanently connected to it?"

I should have stood up to Colin. I'm a firm believer that in life we teach people how to treat us and I unwittingly gave Colin permission to flex his muscles as he recklessly squandered our initial investment. I was later to rue my cowardice when he wanted to push David out. David and I had had a few other warning bells with our third business partner. Whenever things were going well, it was always about what *he'd* done. When they were going badly, it was always the 'royal we', as

David pointed out in one of our management meetings. David oversaw operations and had a better handle on the day-to-day running of the business. It was he who eventually confronted Colin when I was abroad on a business trip. Unfortunately David lost the power struggle and resigned.

While all the backstabbing and politics were playing out, I was gallivanting around the world running the trips, visiting nightclubs and drinking, always drinking. When I wasn't travelling to Berlin or to some other exotic destination, I was in England exploring the underworld club scene and cross-dressing, although I never saw it as that. I went to all manner of clubs. The gay scene and the fetish scene were all broadly accepting of transgendered people whether they were transvestite, transsexual or whatever other mixture. At the same time I felt myself sliding down into an alcoholic oblivion but I couldn't stop.

There is something very exposing about strutting around London in three-inch heels. The wig made me about 6'3". Vulnerable is an understatement. I was a target for any homophobic or transphobic nutcase. One night after leaving 'Heaven', a most inappropriately named nightclub, in the early hours, I was attacked by some skinheads and given a 'good kicking' as one of my attackers yelled as he played football with my head. It was a painful lesson in safety. From then on I never went alone.

All of this was in secret. I hadn't shared my personal revelation with anyone, although five years into our marriage Marie discovered a magazine article about transvestism and transsexuality that I hidden. I had been forced to confess that I liked to wear female clothing on occasion but would confine it to short sessions at home. I wasn't up to telling her the full extent of my feelings and I was still fighting them myself. She had found this peculiar pursuit difficult to understand but I'd managed to convince her that it was harmless and no threat to her. When I wasn't overseas, my work kept me in the office until late but I would seize the opportunity to cross-dress whenever I was in London, Birmingham or Manchester.

It was all supposed to satisfy my yearning to be female but wearing the clothes and going to gay or fetish clubs wasn't exactly 'living in the female gender role' in society and it did little to satisfy me. I resolved to hang on for as long as I could, maybe forever, before actually going ahead and changing my gender role.

The attack made me even more fearful. I was too scared to risk the negative consequences. This denial and avoidance is, I have since found out, very common for trans people. I wish those detractors who think we all make some bizarre lifestyle choice could stand in our shoes for a day before condemning us as perverts or mentally deranged.

The great relief I felt when I finally accepted myself was replaced by depression. Aside from wanting to avoid any change of gender role for the sake of my family, the enormity of the task was overwhelming. There I was, six foot one inch tall or 5' 13" as I'd put it (I still think in old money) with a bass voice and a large masculine nose. Looking skyward, I'd often say, "Give me a break, God, or whoever you are — tall as a lamppost *and* with a deep voice?"

I had brief conversations with God even though I'd given up any notion that He existed. If He did, he certainly wasn't the God of love and compassion my mother was always banging on about.

I'd picked up some major accounts with clients who followed me from my days as an employee and I threw myself into work. I grabbed every foreign trip going. It wasn't uncommon for me to step off a flight from Los Angeles in the morning, drive home from Heathrow, shower, call in to the office and fly off to Hamburg in the evening. I reckoned if I kept moving I'd avoid being in bed with Marie, something that had become more and more difficult. The notion of sex with anyone had become intolerable. And if I was busy or drunk, I didn't have to be with myself either.

I had unlimited access to duty-free alcohol and I used the facility freely, although I never drank in the day or when I was working. As soon as I got home I dived into a bottle, usually gin, my poison of choice. I drank it in a cocktail called a 'Bronx'. My ex-colonial aunt and uncle (my uncle was the Under-Governor of Antigua before Independence) introduced me to it. The drink is one part gin, one part dry Martini vermouth and one part Martini Rosso with a teaspoon of ginger wine, shaken and served over ice with a slice.

I was very good at my job but I was even better at drinking. I'd celebrate with alcohol and drown my sorrows in it. Liza Minnelli summed it up perfectly when she said, "Alcohol is your best friend but it suddenly creeps in through the back door and steals your life."

After the business split when David was ousted, Colin decided he wanted the whole company. He very cynically groomed one of our operations staff and told me he wanted to break away. I wasn't averse to the idea but not on the terms he wanted. Eventually he became more realistic and we settled on a division of clients. Within a few weeks one of the bigger clients had a disastrous travel experience with him and I won them back. But the whole experience of the break-up was draining. I was already in a deteriorating mental state but I resolved to grow the business and secure the future for my family.

Colin turned out to be both ruthless and unscrupulous. I later discovered that he'd paid a private detective to follow me to Lancashire on one of my weekends spent with my trans friend, Helen, in Warrington. When I confronted him, he admitted it was information that he kept up his sleeve in case he ever 'needed it to use against me.'

Despite my personal problems the business grew at a furious rate, almost too quickly. We had a conference division which, with the travel division, had sales managers driving around in BMWs and on expense accounts. I believed I was indestructible and I developed the business in such a way that it could run on its own if I did go ahead and change my gender role. At least, that was the rationale behind my actions. But the problem was I was drinking copious amounts of booze and for the first time it was beginning to affect my work.

I called my drinking my 'Dynasty syndrome' after the popular TV series. I pronounced it in the American style as *die-nasty* which is what I was beginning to do. I'd come home, make one Bronx after the other and drink myself into oblivion before passing out and waking up at four in the morning, slumped on the sofa with empty glasses and bottles lying on the floor. This scenario carried on whenever I was home and not travelling. I had gradually handed over much of the travelling to the staff in preparation for a change of gender, so I could slip into the background. Only one small point, I hadn't found the courage to tell Marie what was going on.

One particular evening, I came home from work and set about getting drunk. I got totally wasted and passed out as usual. I woke up with a jolt. I was lying on the carpet in the lounge. The room was in darkness. The only light was coming from the hall. I felt a heavy weight on my chest. It was Marie, kneeling on me and she was screaming and punching me in the face.

"What's going on? If you don't tell me what's happening I'm leaving. Are you seeing another woman?"

"Yes, I am!" I said, grabbing her arms to fend off the attack.

She sat back with a wounded look on her face. She was unprepared for my answer. She began to stand up to leave the room.

"It's me," I said quietly. "I'm the other woman. It's me."

"What?" She stared at me, an incredulous expression on her face.

"I'm transsexual," I slurred. I broke down and sobbed uncontrollably. All the years of suppression and secrecy flooded out of me like an alcoholic tidal wave of relief and I just let it go.

"So wearing the clothes isn't enough then?" Marie was still staring at me.

"No. It was never just the clothes," I said wearily.

We talked over a cup of tea and I told her everything. She was stunned and although she knew I had cross-dressed, she said she'd always suspected it was more than just dressing up.

"So what do we do now?" Marie asked. Dawn broke as I told her I was willing to get treatment to see what could be done. This amazing woman turned to me and said, "Let's get an appointment with a specialist."

And we began an amazing journey of pain, sorrow, joy and a deep exploration of ourselves.

I knew who to contact to get help. It was the only person in London outside of the NHS who specialised in this field. I called Dr R's office the next day and made an appointment. I figured after waiting over thirty years, a six-week wait wasn't the end of the world.

Oddly enough, my first appointment was at Ealing Hospital, the former Hanwell Lunatic Asylum, the very place Marie's father had died a horrible slow death years earlier. We agreed it would be too stressful for her to go and I went on my own.

As I made my way across the grounds to a converted Nissen hut, the semi-circular roofed building seen on old airfields, I became aware of the patients standing around me outdoors who were all clearly very ill. They had the gaunt, vacant facial expressions people get when they're dissociating from the world. Some were muttering to themselves, many were rocking their bodies backwards and forward whilst others just stared into space.

"Well, this confirms it. You're well and truly mad!" I muttered to myself as I made my way into the doctor's office.

Gender Dysphoria and Gender Identity Disorder, as it used to be labelled by clinicians in the mental health field, isn't something that can be diagnosed by others. It's a self-diagnosed condition, if *condition* is the appropriate adjective. I've never believed clinicians really know how to work with patients in this field. They just become gatekeepers, reduced to observation roles, there to try and stop anyone from making drastic mistakes or finishing themselves off.

There was nothing for me to really *get* from this first appointment. I already knew what the answer was and it wasn't more aversion therapy or a cure. To my surprise the doctor agreed with me and offered me female hormones as the only solution. But he told me he'd only prescribe them if I reduced my alcohol intake. I had promised Marie I'd make no decisions without her and so I made a second appointment a few weeks later with the same doctor, but in a different location. In the meantime I went cold turkey and stopped drinking.

At the follow-up meeting the doctor explained to Marie that oestrogen in small doses might calm me down and that it wouldn't induce irreversible changes. Marie and I had already discussed the possibility of taking hormones and I'd expressed my desire to at least make a start.

Twenty-four hours later I swallowed my first purple hormone pill and the lengthy process of changing my body began. I went to bed that night feeling a cocktail of emotions. I was relieved that at long last I was doing something positive, but I also knew my life was entering its most challenging phase. What was going to happen to my wife, my children and me?

The medication was supposed to help me to see how I felt. Hormones reassured me that at some undefined time in the future I'd finally be released from my prison. Taking them was the first step to permanent change.

That night I had the best night's sleep in years. And I needed all the strength I could muster for what lay ahead. Blissfully, I was ignorant of the details.

8
STEPPING OUT:
MY GUARDIAN
ANGEL SHOWS UP

"It's never too late to be what you might have been."
George Eliot

—————◦○◦—————

George Orwell's *1984* wasn't a book I'd particularly enjoyed reading as a child. My friends and I were all fashionably left-wing at the time and frequently debated the likely future accuracy of 'Big Brother' and 'the Police State'. It was ironic that I was beginning a process that might lead to me breaking out from the prison that was my body in that very same year of 1984.

The hormone-induced changes to my body were very gradual. I felt a tingling sensation behind my nipples but couldn't see any signs of breast growth. I became weepy at times but I couldn't see any signs of feminisation to my face or body. I've since learned that trans women always have unrealistic expectations of the feminising effect of hormone therapy as the oestrogen, even with an androgen or testosterone suppressant, struggles to compete with the more powerful testosterone. Changes are frustratingly gradual.

Oestrogen is unable to change the cranial features of a natal male face. For this reason trans women are more visible in society. Most people believe there are more trans women (male to female trans people) than trans men (female to males) but it's not the case. It's just that trans men take testosterone which masculinises the face and body thus often enabling them to integrate more easily, at least on an outward appearance level.

In 1984 I was oblivious to this information about the effects of hormones and despite my masculine appearance I felt relieved that I'd at least taken steps toward the possibility of change. I began electrolysis, the painful removal of my facial hair, one hair at a time and was able to cover my fair beard with make-up fairly easily. What I still hadn't done in 1984 was venture out in public. Going to transvestite or gay clubs where tolerance and acceptance were assured was one thing, but out and about in daylight presented a very different challenge.

One sunny summer afternoon I decided to be brave and do some window shopping in London's Oxford Street as a woman. I donned a simple white calf-length denim skirt, a plain pink top with a polo neck to hide my Adam's apple, low-heeled, navy court shoes and a matching handbag. I applied my daytime makeup with care and topped everything off with my new shoulder-length wig.

"If you're going to do it, do it in style," I thought. I jumped in my car and sped off to minimise the risk of being seen by any nosey neighbours. I drove to London, stopping at traffic lights so I was slightly behind the cars in adjacent lanes, just in case the drivers looked sideways and realised I wasn't a 'real' woman.

I parked the car in Manchester Square a few hundred yards from Oxford Street and was suddenly gripped with fear. What if everyone pointed at me or laughed at my ludicrous appearance? What if I was attacked by a bunch of skinheads again? These thoughts raced through my mind as I took one last look at my makeup in the mirror and opened the car door. Feeling the air on my legs I strode off, shoulders back, heart pounding, in the direction of the shops.

My first test arrived. Someone was walking towards me. But they passed by without even noticing me. I passed the point where it would have been easier to turn back than to carry on, past the point of no return. It was a perfect metaphor for my life.

I strode towards the hubbub of Oxford Street and entered Selfridges. For the first time I looked through rails of clothes without worrying what the sales assistant thought. I continued along Oxford Street and entered several fashion shops. After a couple of hours I headed back to the car.

I opened the car door and sat down, slamming the door as though it was a punch in the air. I'd done it and people hadn't stared or pointed. I had not spoken to anyone but that challenge was for another day. I cried with joy. I knew my dream would one day be a reality. The genie was well and truly out of the bottle. There really was no going back.

I confided in my closest friend Valerie that I was embarking on a road that may lead to transition. She was upset for me and for what I'd been struggling with and she was also immensely supportive. Valerie suggested we have a day out together so I'd feel safer with another person to accompany me. Only a close friend who really cares about me would embark on what could have been a very difficult journey with me. Time and time again she would prove that she was my guardian angel.

A week later I was back in the West End and we had lunch in St Christopher's Place near Bond Street. We looked around the shops. This time I was aware of one or two stares and nudges but by and large nobody took much notice.

Next we went to London Zoo. Children are notoriously honest and open. Teenage girls are interested in their development and they are conscious of grown women. They notice their mannerisms and appearance. As we were walking around the zoo, a group of schoolgirls in uniform headed our way. Oh God! Would they shriek and point? Again nothing, I was totally ignored. I didn't want the day to end. I was enjoying every moment and I felt totally liberated.

"I haven't seen you look this happy in ages," Valerie remarked as we drove home, marking the passing of another landmark.

Over the next few months my small breasts began to grow. The electrolysis had advanced to the point where I'd stopped shaving altogether and my hair had grown to a length which meant I no longer needed a wig.

I had a perm. The curls were smaller than I'd requested. I feared that I would look like Kevin Keegan and the many British footballers who sported horrid perms in the 1980s, but it meant I could gel my hair flat during the day, come home, wash it and allow it to spring into a feminine style without any great effort, before going out in the evening.

A year after my first visit to the psychiatrist, Marie and I faced up to the possibility of a permanent change of gender role. Marie and my female self had spent time out together. I didn't need to say anything to her. She could see there was no turning back. We had a lot of decisions to make. Would we stay together? What about the children? Should I leave home?

I was liberated by expressing my female self but I had no delusions about living full-time in the female role and the difficulty of running a business as a woman. Apart from the fact that my voice was very masculine, I'd only spent time as a female in a social context and then only with a few people I knew and trusted.

Marie and I agreed that I should work toward transition. I couldn't cope with struggling in a male role for much longer. The first job was to tell the children. The risk of them seeing their father dressed in women's clothes was more likely with my increasing need to express myself fully. They'd already seen the perm when it wasn't gelled down but convincing them it was just my 'Kevin Keegan' phase was getting difficult.

We took advice and discussed, at great length, the possible effect on the girls. We reasoned that the love of two parents was better than only one. At the same time we recognised it might become difficult for them at school with their peers. I decided if it caused them too much upset, I'd move out.

When the time came, we decided it was better if Marie broke the news to them. We thought it might be easier for them to ask questions and feel less embarrassed if I wasn't around. Marie would pick a suitable moment, if there ever can be such a thing for such a massive piece of information for a child.

One weekend I was up in my bedroom working on the computer. I'd long since moved out of the marital bed and into the spare room which doubled as a bedroom and study. I heard footsteps approaching the door. Marie came in with the two girls, who were holding her hands.

"The girls have something to tell you," she said.

Laura spoke first. "Mummy told us you're going to be a lady but we want you to stay."

They both ran to me and threw their arms around my neck and I wept. It was the greatest expression of love any human being could ever receive.

"There's one condition," Laura added. "We want to choose your new name."

That seemed the cheapest price anyone could possibly pay for such love and Michelle was officially named. It didn't escape my notice that it was Laura's middle name. Susie presumably lost out in the debate. I have often been accused of being cruel by putting my children through this experience. They were only three and six years old when this conversation occurred. There's no way I can defend or justify what I did. In a sense my decisions were very selfish. Of course I regret the pain I put my family through.

But would it have been easier if I had left home? The children would still have been stigmatised at school and anyway, we all loved each other. I can't defend my decision other than to say that life had become intolerable and I did what I felt compelled to do.

As adults, both girls now say the fact they were given a choice and were involved in the decision rather than having it imposed upon them made it easier for them. All I know is I'm the luckiest person alive to have benefitted from the love of such an amazing family. My family saved my life. They really did.

I set about preparing for the momentous day when my life would change. I had rhinoplasty to feminise my large nose and surgery to reduce my Adam's apple.

I have no idea how she told her but Marie's mother got the news that her son-in-law was going to become her daughter-in-law.

"Do you plan to continue to take care of your family?" she asked me the next time I saw her.

I was surprised by her question but confirmed that I would. She surprised me further by offering her spare room if ever the pressure on the family got too great and if disappearing for a while would help. All she wanted to know was that her daughter was ok. It was another illustration of love.

I carried on for another year or so in this no-man's-land, popping hormones, electrolysis and planning for the eventual transition. My main objective was to get my travel business, Creative Destinations, into a position where it could function, with me in the background. I feared a backlash from clients and I didn't want to jeopardise the future of the business. I thought withdrawing would take the heat out of the situation. The problem was I was employing two people to bring in new business and they simply weren't doing it.

The cost of running expensive company cars and paying out salaries that were a drain rather than an investment was beginning to take its toll on the business and on me. In his excellent book, *E-myth Revisited,* Michael Gerber talks about the need for a business to be able to run without the owner. How right he is.

Profits were suffering and the prospect of me stepping back receded. The longer it went on like this, the more depressed I became and the more frustrated I felt. We were busy but we were not productive and we were haemorrhaging money. I started drinking again and began losing confidence in my ability to transition successfully. It wasn't helped by a couple of incidents when my safety was threatened and my cover blown.

Valerie and her husband Tony were great supports. The four of us went for meals or drinks where I could express myself fully in the female role. On one such occasion we were eating a meal in a London restaurant. A group of drunken guys sat at the next table and the elbow nudging began. This was followed by verbal insults as they taunted the 'tranny'.

We left the restaurant before finishing our meal. My companions did their best to reassure me it was a one-off and that I looked fine. But their attempts at reassurance did nothing to lift my depression. If I couldn't 'pass' in a restaurant, how the hell would I survive in a work environment?

Despite this setback I went to the same restaurant the following night on my own. I needed to conquer my fear and prove to myself I could overcome the insults of a few morons. I had to get back on the horse. This philosophy of getting up when I'm knocked down continues to serve me well. My 'never say die' attitude is in my DNA – it is a gift from my father. I was to need it more than even *I* realised at that time. This sort of aggressive experience was fortunately quite rare and it decreased as time went on and my confidence in my ability to survive grew.

I had other supportive friends. On my regular business trips to Manchester I had become friendly with a small group of trans girls. Jennifer was already living full time as a woman, and in 'stealth' as the Americans very descriptively put it when someone has fully integrated. John wasn't sure whether he would move forward and Helen was just about to begin living fully in the female role.

Helen knew how important support was and she made a point of going out with me to pubs and clubs in Manchester. I must have looked a little suspect to say the least around this time but Helen knew it was a phase you have to live through. She befriended me through it. We remained friends until 2000 when I discovered through her partner that she had died suddenly after a massive stroke. Trans women take hormones knowing that there's an increased risk of breast and liver cancer as well as strokes but I didn't for one moment think that Helen would die so suddenly at the age of thirty-nine. It was a great loss. Her parents excluded her trans friends from the funeral so I was unable to attend.

Despite my problems I was beginning to feel happier about my body. To my relief my hated male genitalia became incapable of functioning and I could blank it from my mind. I had my second surgical procedure, a lip enhancement. I was conscious of owning very thin masculine lips and I wanted to feminise them. After the surgery the stitches around my mouth made me resemble the Bride of Freddie Krueger. Worse still, the operation failed to deliver the feminine lips I so desired. I felt the fee was wasted and my finances were dwindling fast.

9
DESPERATION AND DESPAIR

"Desperation is the raw material of drastic change. Only those who can leave behind everything they have ever believed in can hope to escape."
William S. Burroughs

————◦◦◦————

Business was tough and I'd gone back to escorting the most important overseas groups. When we were planning an event, we usually took a representative from the client company on a reconnaissance visit or 'recce' as they were known.

On one such occasion we were planning a two-centre trip to Orlando and Longboat Key near Sarasota in Florida. It was an upmarket trip for senior executives so the accommodation needed to be 5 star. For the five-day recce I flew out to Tampa with my client and his wife to finalise the arrangements. I was worried about the future and depressed about everything. I was not sleeping well and my alcohol intake rose to dangerous levels again.

During the flight to Tampa the three of us had a fair bit to drink and I arrived tired and hung-over. We took a cab to the delightful resort of Longboat Key which has since become one of my favourite resorts in the US. En route I realised I had no cash. We stopped off at a supermarket and I bought a half bottle of Jack Daniels with a travellers cheque and got the change in cash.

It was late evening by the time we arrived at our hotel and since we had eaten well in Business Class on our flight we went straight to our rooms. It was a lovely place but I barely noticed my surroundings as I opened the bottle of Jack Daniels and set about liberating its contents. I went to bed drunk and exhausted, but I couldn't sleep. I was tormented by the fear on the one hand of losing everything when I transitioned and the unimaginable option of *not* transitioning on the other. At around four a.m. I left my luxurious condominium and went for a walk.

Longboat Key is a long sandbar on Florida's Gulf Coast. It is a favourite resort for well-heeled Americans and in those days it was relatively unknown to overseas tourists. I set off for a stroll along the fine sandy beach. It was a balmy night. A half-moon glinted on the still ocean. After a few hundred yards I came upon a dock or pier jutting out to sea. I walked along it to the water's edge some twenty yards from the shore and looked down into the dark water. It was lapping at the wooden stilts holding up the structure, just above sea level. It couldn't have been more than twenty feet deep but it was deep enough. The dark water was inviting. I didn't want to die, but I wanted to stop living.

I decided to let the waters consume me, let them take all the pain away. I lowered myself down to the edge and said sorry to Marie and the children.

"Hey, are you OK?"

I turned to see an early morning jogger, a young man in his late twenties, silhouetted by the moonlight on the shore.

"I'm fine," I replied weakly.

I stepped back from the edge and turned again towards my knight in shining armour but there was no one there. Was I drunk and hallucinating? Did I imagine it? Was it an angel from heaven?

I lurched back towards the sandy beach. A gentle breeze chilled the tears that flowed down my cheeks. I felt the fine, warm sand under my feet and I sank to my knees and broke down into uncontrollable sobs. I vomited and rid myself of most of the Jack Daniels.

"Please God, take this pain away and free me," I cried.

"What's the point?" I thought aloud. "There's no God. It's a waste of time asking."

I staggered back to my temporary home in the Colony Resort and collapsed on the bed. I managed to pull myself together and somehow got through the rest of the trip.

On my return I phoned my local Samaritan branch where I'd been working as a volunteer and resigned. It was no good having suicidal volunteers taking calls from suicidal callers. I felt myself losing control of my business and my destiny. I stayed sober for long enough to get me through the working day but I was withdrawn and wasn't supporting my staff. As pressure grew from the bank I began to think I couldn't carry through my change of gender role. It just felt impossible.

I didn't even bother to hide the extent of my evening drinking from Marie anymore. Life had become a round of working long hours in the office or flying somewhere with clients. When I was home, I drank and went to bed with little prospect of sleeping. My mind was in torment. One Saturday, a few weeks after Longboat Key, I spent the day in an empty office poring over the figures. They didn't look good. We were weeks from bankruptcy.

At home that evening Marie announced she was going to bed early. I sat looking into space and again decided I had had enough. I sat down at the computer and typed out two letters. One for Valerie and one for Marie. I sealed the envelopes and left them in the kitchen.

I poured a mixture of gin and tonic water into a large pint glass and swallowed a packet of Paracetamol down with it. I knew from my experience with the Samaritans that Paracetemol and alcohol make a fatal cocktail. Even if you survive the first twelve hours the liver fails over the next few days. I don't remember passing out but I do remember vomiting while on all fours in the kitchen.

But suddenly, I didn't want to die. I never had. I just didn't want to live anymore, which wasn't quite the same thing. I gulped down a couple of pints of water from the tap and made myself sick again, but this time in the sink. I should have gone to hospital but I was certain I'd only passed out for a few moments and had rid myself of the pills. I hadn't done any lasting damage.

Marie heard the noise and came downstairs to see what was going on. The look on her face told its own story. She'd had enough too, enough of me being depressed and miserable. She read the note.

"Next time do it properly, or I'll finish the job for you." She had tears in her eyes as she stormed out of the room.

The following evening Valerie dropped in unexpectedly.

"You look terrible. What's happened?" She looked at me aghast.

I broke down. "I just can't go on, it's hopeless."

I told her what had happened. Marie had already shown her the note. Valerie thrust a bag at me.

"Read this. I bought it for you. You need to stop feeling sorry for yourself and pull yourself together."

She turned on her heel and walked to the door. "I'll ring you," she said. Valerie was my guardian angel. Without her support the whole thing would have been so much harder. In fact I don't know if I'd have survived without her love and support as well as from my immediate family.

In the bag was a copy of *The Prophet* by Kahlil Gibran. I'd never heard of it until then but I since discovered that it has been read by millions around the world. As I read it, the realisation struck me that the words felt too powerful, too spiritual, to have been written by any human. Each chapter mesmerised me. It was as though the chapter beginning, 'Your joy is your sorrow unmasked' had been written specifically for me.

It finally dawned on me that my experience could have a positive side. The problem was that I was stuck and I had lost sight of my vision and the bigger picture. But there was hope. I started to be able to see it. With love, there is always hope. The book made me question my beliefs and I began to explore my spirituality by reading everything I could lay my hands on.

I read a biography of Gibran and discovered that I really didn't like the man. This fuelled my belief that the words in *The Prophet* were coming through him but they weren't his words. I also realised that if I had been so angry with God for so long, maybe God really *was* out there somewhere. Maybe he or she did exist.

Valerie is a medium, or more accurately, a Christian Spiritualist. She suggested that I might one day like a reading although not with her because she knew too much about me. Instead she recommended one of her peers from the psychic world. Marie and I agreed we would both go for individual readings.

The medium was a lady in her late fifties or early sixties with an air of deep concentration although her face betrayed little expression. We sat at a table and she explained that she would go into a deep relaxed space and wait to see if she got any messages. She said she would only tell me what she got but wouldn't interpret anything for me. It was up to me to interpret the message for myself.

I was feeling vulnerable and was pretty resistant to the process but I was willing to give it a try. My cynicism wasn't lessened by the opening encounter. She held my hands and after a few moments her body shuddered.

I thought, "Oh no, here we go. If there's a knock under the table and she asks, 'Is there anybody there?' I swear, I'll walk out!"

But what she actually said stopped me in my tracks.

She looked up at me. "There's a war going on in your mind."

I couldn't have described how I felt any more eloquently. She now had my attention.

What happened next blew me away. She told me she was getting a picture of a garden with lots of roses in the flower beds, bordering a well-kept lawn. The garden was on two levels with a birdbath in the middle. The hairs stood up on the back of my neck. When she described a separate garden fenced off at the bottom with a gate as a fruit garden and not an orchard, I knew for sure she was describing Granny Cooper's garden in Ealing.

It was as though I'd come home. I began to weep.

The medium continued. "I can see an old lady sitting on the step. She has grey hair in a bun and she's wearing a wrap-over pinafore sitting on the step, with a pile of fruit in her lap."

By now I was in bits. She continued. "In the kitchen there's a big, old-fashioned stove that heats the water and the house. There's a little boy sitting on the stove with a bowl of custard with fruit, blackberries I think. He's stirring the contents and making patterns with the blackberries in the custard. It's you, isn't it?" she asked. "This old lady is your grandmother, isn't she?"

I nodded through the tears.

"She wants me to tell you she'll be with you on whichever path you choose and not to be afraid."

By the end of the session my head was spinning. I'd heard everything that had been said but I couldn't take it in. I didn't really believe in all this spiritual mumbo jumbo but there was absolutely no way this woman could have known about that garden, about Granny or about the fruit. It must have been real.

On a separate visit Marie got a message describing her situation as 'wearing a pair of golden handcuffs'. She said it described perfectly the way she was feeling. Marie often described our situation as a 'hurricane' with me in the eye of the storm. I had control over my decisions but she was on the fringes, reaping the effects of the winds of change. I think in many ways the whole thing was harder for her than it was for me.

10
TELLING MY FAMILY

*"Change only occurs when one becomes who one is and
not who one is not."*
Arnold Beisser

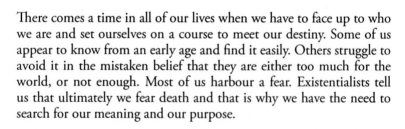

There comes a time in all of our lives when we have to face up to who we are and set ourselves on a course to meet our destiny. Some of us appear to know from an early age and find it easily. Others struggle to avoid it in the mistaken belief that they are either too much for the world, or not enough. Most of us harbour a fear. Existentialists tell us that ultimately we fear death and that is why we have the need to search for our meaning and our purpose.

Like millions of others I was inspired by Viktor Frankl who wrote *Man's Search For Meaning*, a work born of his experience as an inmate in Auschwitz. Frankl argues that while we often can't change the circumstance in which we find ourselves, we always have a choice about how we respond to it.

As well as volunteering with the Samaritans, it was reading Frankl that sowed the seeds of my interest in psychology and psychotherapy which I later studied. I learned that if we feel abandoned, we fear the world will reject us and if our parents don't trust us to make our own decisions early enough, we feel we are inadequate.

At the time I was facing up to *my* truth. I certainly felt that who I was, was way too much for the world but I wasn't brave enough to cope with it. I had a double whammy of insecurity. Whatever the journey, I don't believe it's too much for any of us. But what we so often fail to realise is that we cannot do it on our own. We need to tap into a greater power and we forget there are people who love us. Fear itself is irrational. We get desperate about what *might* happen long before the reality. And the reality is rarely as bad as we imagine. Statistics from the Samaritans show that young people kill themselves before exams in the belief that they are failures. But rarely does anyone kill themselves *after* receiving the results, even if they *have* failed.

After years of inching my way towards transition, Marie and I agreed a provisional date for me to start living in the female gender role full-time. We gave ourselves time to sort out various things at work and for me to tell my sisters before telling my parents. None of them had an inkling of my situation, let alone my future plans. I contacted my sisters, Penny and Geraldine (Dina as she later preferred to be called), and told them I had something very important to tell them. They were intrigued, the meeting was set and we met at Geraldine's house.

I'd recently read what, in the late eighties, I thought was the best book on the subject of transsexuality, *Bodyshock* by Liz Hodgkinson. Thirty years later the forests of the world continue to be depleted in order to accommodate the world's insatiable appetite for what is seen as a bizarre and intriguing subject.

Back then, anyone 'changing sex' as it was inappropriately called was seen as a freak of Nature and it made headlines in the tabloid press. My intention was to give my sisters a copy of the book to help them understand where I was coming from. When I arrived at the house in leafy Chesham Bois near Amersham, my sisters were already waiting.

"Tea or coffee?" asked Geraldine.

"I'm fine." I began what I wanted to say. "Did you ever think I was different when we were kids?" I asked them.

They both shook their heads as if to say 'get to the point'.

"You know, I never felt happy growing up as a boy," I said. And I told them what had been happening to me and what was about to happen. I said I hoped they would support our parents when I broke the news to them. They asked dozens of questions.

"What about Marie?"

"What about the children?"

"What about work?"

At the end of the conversation I offered the book to either one of them suggesting they forward it on to the other.

"You take it. I'll buy a copy," Geraldine said quickly, passing it to Penny.

"You look shell-shocked, Penny," I said to my sister who looked deep in thought.

She slowly shook her head and remained tight-lipped. We agreed that I would let them know when I was going to tell our parents and we parted agreeing to speak on the phone within a few days.

I had several more conversations with Geraldine. She, her partner Alan, Marie and I went out for a meal together to discuss the situation. It was the first time she had seen her brother looking more like a sister.

"Your makeup looks great," she said with a curious smile.

"I've been practising for years," I said. "You just never knew it."

But Penny was silent. Days led to weeks. Eventually, I wrote and asked if she'd finished with the book. It arrived in the mail a few days later with no letter or note. When I opened it, I saw a piece of paper which had obviously been used as a bookmark, about six pages in.

With the exception of my parents' funerals and on one other occasion, I haven't seen her since. My nieces' weddings, the births of their children and various family gatherings have come and gone without invitations being extended. Once I asked a family member why me and my family weren't invited to my eldest niece's wedding. I was told Penny had said, "And who am I supposed to say he is?"

Perhaps the truth was too shaming for her? What goes on in someone's life that makes them so insecure they would rather cut their brother out of their lives than face the embarrassment of what the neighbours might think? I think losing her brother as she saw it was too much for her. I was taken by surprise by my sister's reaction but it helped prepare me for the broader rejection to follow.

On three different occasions I went to see my parents to tell them but the words wouldn't come out. I'd go armed with a plan but was thwarted by fear or just feeling the timing wasn't right. Eventually after two pints of Guinness in a nearby pub, the moment came. I can't remember the exact words I used but I do remember breaking down as I told them.

"What did we do wrong?" my mother asked, comforting me.

"Nothing, Mum. It just happens."

"But it isn't normal!" she exclaimed.

"You're right there, Mum!" I quipped through my tears.

It was the first of only two occasions in my life when I saw my father cry. The other was after my mother died. I felt his tears were saying, 'I've lost my son.' I left feeling wretched. I was destroying my family in my pursuit of peace of mind. It wasn't helped by the fact that my mother had become unwell. She had developed a small lump in her stomach and was scheduled for exploratory surgery in the February.

Who else to tell?

I was advised only to tell people on a need-to-know basis and shortly before the change itself. That way they have less time to start imagining some kind of horror show. For that reason I kept it to my family and Valerie. The only other person I told was my friend, Aitor, in Melbourne in a letter. I reasoned Australia was too far away to worry about.

Aitor, the friend from Ladbrokes with whom I had travelled to France with on our excursion to Le Mans, is a real man's man, always playing around with cars and his beloved Ferraris. I posted the letter just before Christmas. One night in between Christmas and New Year the phone rang in the early hours. He clearly hadn't worked out the time difference. I could hear him choking back the emotion as he told me how privileged he felt that I'd told him first. He wished me well and our friendship continued.

Aitor's reaction was the first to illustrate that men who are comfortable with their sexuality and with their identity are fine about it. It was the men who boasted in the pub that they had 'screwed' this woman or that secretary who seemed to struggle with it and became verbally, even physically, aggressive.

11

ATTACKED:
NOTHING LIKE TRAVEL TO
BROADEN THE MIND

"Your joy is your sorrow unmasked."
Kahlil Gibran

———————◦◦◦———————

In January 1991 I escorted my last trip abroad in the male gender role. It was one of my best clients and I decided to lead the trip to Rio de Janeiro. The event nearly didn't happen because our clients wouldn't pay the large sums needed for the trip after their accountants had discovered the perilous state of our finances. They insisted on paying airlines and hotels direct. I was worried about our suppliers finding out how rocky we'd become but I reluctantly complied with their request.

It was always one of my ambitions to explore the Inca culture and Machu Picchu, the fabled lost city of the Incas in Peru. Earlier visits to Mexico had whetted my appetite. We'd never taken large groups to Peru because the country's infrastructure was poor and crime was high. Shining Path guerrillas were kidnapping western businessmen for ransom and inflation was running at over one hundred percent, so it made it impossible to cost a complex travel arrangement months before a trip. Brazil was a much easier sell and a far simpler proposition. Having seen my clients off on their trip back to England, I made ready for the flight to Peru.

If you've never flown to the capital Lima, you can't possibly imagine the chaos at the airport. The arrival lounge was a teeming mass of humanity. Taxi drivers, hotel reps, meet-and-greet representatives, friends and families, all fought each other just to move forward a few feet. It was as though they were screaming to get to the last lifeboat on the Titanic.

Being tall I managed to see my name on one of the many nameboards and scraps of paper being held up by the representatives. My agent, Rafael, took my suitcase and told me I must follow him and not stray more than a foot away. His instructions sounded bizarre until we left the relative safety of the arrival lounge and stepped out into the night.

Soldiers with machine guns stood outside the building to prevent the hundreds of hustlers and beggars from getting into the terminal. It's easy to be critical but at the end of the eighties and early nineties this was a country on the brink of economic collapse with little or no welfare state. The average Peruvian was struggling to survive and wealthy 'gringos' — as all westerners were assumed to be — were a potential source of income.

We drove into Lima and I checked into my hotel. Again, it was heavily guarded by uniformed machine-gun-toting officers patrolling the lobby. I went to bed and prepared for my flight to the ancient town of Cusco the following day.

There the temperature dropped dramatically. The rarity of the air was what really hit me. High in the Andes, it is common for visitors to become exhausted and fall ill from altitude sickness. The Peruvians have a cure in the form of coca tea. The leaves of the coca plant provide a stimulant which relaxes and mitigates the sickness. Many locals chewed the leaves and had a perpetual stoned look about them.

I took a guided tour of the area, taking snaps of the children herding their llamas or alpacas. Every time we stepped off the coach we were faced with children begging. I took a photograph of a little girl of no more than seven or eight holding her hands out. It was only when the photographs had been developed that I saw the pained eyes and a forlorn expression on her face. I ignored her pleas for help and I have felt guilty about it ever since. It was a callous gesture which I deeply regret. It is as though I had denied Jesus himself.

The next day I awoke early and decided to go for a walk. It was daylight and I thought if I stayed around the town centre, what could possibly go wrong? It was a chilly, grey morning. The cobbled streets were wet from overnight rain as I walked around the square and headed past a school, where some smartly dressed children in school uniforms were chattering noisily before their daily lessons. As I walked past, one of them pointed at my watch, beckoning for me to tell her the time.

"Ocho y medio," I told her. Half past eight. She appeared not to hear me and encouraged me to lean over so that she could see my watch. Quick as lightning I felt a hand grab my hair from behind and wrench my head back. Then a fist punched me in the throat. Someone's arm had me by the neck in a headlock. A third man grabbed my arms and a fourth rifled my pockets. I couldn't draw breath and I was choking. I thought I was going to die.

I knew not to wear flashy jewellery or expensive clothes. My wedding ring was on a chord around my neck hidden by a high-necked sweater. I felt my wristwatch being taken and my leather jacket was stripped from me as I started to lose consciousness.

I kicked out at one of my assailants in front of me. My left foot connected with his jaw. I heard a click as my foot slammed into the side of his face. He staggered back with a yelp and his face turned red with rage. He bent down and picked up a piece of concrete about the size of a grapefruit. Attached to his hand, I saw it coming towards my face as he grunted, "Gringo!"

I don't know for how long I was unconscious. It was probably no more than a couple of minutes. I became aware of an icy, cold wet stone on my face and the pool of warm blood I was lying in. The blood was spreading its way from my nose across the cobbled road and into the gutter. I became aware of something fiddling with my feet. I looked down. It was an old woman trying to steal my shoes. I uttered something and kicked out. Startled, she ran off.

I raised my head. I couldn't feel my nose. When I put my hand to my face, it felt as though my nose had gone or had spread itself flat. My hands and clothes were covered in blood. I had read stories of people having their fingers chopped off to get wedding rings but then I remembered I'd hidden mine.

I looked around to find people standing there and staring but nobody came forward to help me. Holding my nose, or what I assumed was still my nose, to stem the flow of blood, I got to my feet and staggered down the road towards the market. Just as in boxing, the body doesn't feel the pain at the time of the violence, only later. My nervous system kicked in. My head was pounding, my nose was throbbing and my throat became agony.

The violence and intensity of the attack reminded me of the assault a few years earlier in London. This attack was more violent and made worse by the fact that it was executed with such hatred by my assailants. As I reached the pharmacy near my hotel, the sky began to spin and I passed out again. When I awoke, I was back at my hotel with a doctor and my agent standing over me.

Apparently someone from the hotel was walking by just a few yards away from the pharmacy and had seen me. My agent dropped everything to come over and get help. My nose was broken but it hadn't spread across my face as I'd first thought and the doctor reset it with his forefinger and thumb. Thankfully, I wasn't fully conscious at the time. I was given a strong sedative and slept for several hours.

Later that evening I went by taxi to the Army HQ which doubled as a Police HQ, where I was asked to make a statement. The officer showed me a large book of mug shots and asked if I could identify anyone. This was a ludicrous proposition since all the men in the photos had panda-like black eyes and plasters across their noses, rendering identification impossible. Evidently it was common practice for arrested suspects to be rifle-butted before questioning. Great! Now I looked like a suspect too!

The one thing I had remembered, aside from the vivid image of my friend with the piece of concrete, was that the two men were both wearing blue sweaters. This turned out to be part of the attire worn by off-duty soldiers. I decided not to take my complaint any further.

The next day I awoke with a thumping headache but I felt better. I looked into the mirror and saw two black eyes peeking out over a swollen, blue nose, with a large sticking plaster over it. I showered, dressed and went down to breakfast. I ate in the corner of the restaurant to avoid the stares of the other tourists.

Today was the day. I was booked to go by train to Machu Picchu and then through the Andes to Puno, one of the world's greatest train journeys. Better on this train than in a hotel room licking my wounds. When I'm travelling, I'm always at peace with the world. I'm a restless spirit, only ever truly happy on the move.

From the train we boarded a coach for the last leg of the journey up the lush green mountainside to the lost city. To my astonishment I bumped into Julie, one of my travel industry peers. She was on holiday with her mother and after all the usual 'Fancy meeting you here' exchanges and 'What happened to your face?' we went our separate ways, agreeing to have lunch back in England.

Like most people, I'd seen pictures of the ruins and of the famous green sugar-loaf-shaped mountain and ruins at Machu Picchu but to actually be there was very special. I sat down in a peaceful spot among the ruins away from the few tourists who were around. I closed my eyes and I prayed. I wasn't too sure about God but I knew something was out there. I prayed hard. A couple of hours must have passed but I was oblivious to time. I sat there and wept. I emptied myself of all the tears of self-pity, all the anger, all the frustration and all the hurt. I felt changed. Something had clicked inside me and I felt a vigour that I hadn't felt in ages and an optimism I don't think I'd *ever* felt before. Something else was different too. Now I had strength. I couldn't call myself a Christian or a believer of any other faith, but my spirit felt refreshed.

Then, broken nose and all, I climbed part of the way up the 'green sugar loaf' as it's known. The air was thin and my face and limbs ached. Gulping for breath, I made it a good way up before being forced to turn back on the advice of a guide who warned that the weather was closing in.

The train journey from Machu Picchu to Puno on the edge of Lake Titicaca is sensational. One beautiful vista after another passes by the window as the train chugs its way through the snow-capped Andes. It's rightly known as one of the great train journeys of the world and for good reason. The train passed through terrain as varied as it was stunning. The mountain peaks gave way to plains interrupted by villages awash with muddy streets from the recent rains.

I struck up a stilted conversation in broken Spanish with the occasional 'grazie' or 'prego' thrown in with two Italian tourists. The meal on the train was an experience in itself. The choice was chicken, chicken or chicken, so I went for the chicken. As one waiter placed the dish in front of me, another followed with a sauceboat containing a thick pink sauce resembling a thickened Thousand Island dressing.

"Sin salsa, gracias," I said hurriedly as the waiter leaned over me. No sauce thanks! Five minutes later another waiter came past and proceeded to cover my chicken in the offending gunge before I could stop him. Pink gunge seemed to be compulsory. I picked at the food. Thankfully my blocked nose rendered it tasteless.

My overnight stop was in a small town called Juliaca before heading off to Puno and over the lake to Bolivia. Dusk was descending as the train prepared to enter the town. The staff on the train pulled the blinds down to reduce the risk of the carriage being stoned, as the poverty-stricken locals took out their frustration on us wealthy 'gringos' (foreigners). It is easy to think of some of those people as thugs but it's worth remembering they blamed the US for its desperate economic woes at that time. And it wasn't without foundation, hence the 'gringo' insult while I was being mugged.

Upon arrival in Juliaca we were instructed to run the few yards from the station to the bus. We then drove a few miles to the hotel in Puno. One of the regular power failures occurred and I slept on the floor propped up against a chair, which I, in turn, propped up against the door. The lock on my door wasn't working properly, the safety chain was flimsy and I didn't feel safe. I didn't want to be mugged again.

Puno is on the shore of Lake Titicaca and is probably most famous for the images of the indigenous Indian women wearing bowler hats or 'Crown Derbys' as the locals called them. I spent the morning with some English tourists I'd bumped into. You can guess what sort of conversation ensued.

"Oooh, what happened to your face?" "Where did it happen?" My response then sparked off a series of anecdotes heard third-hand from other tourists who'd similarly fallen foul of local villains. One dramatic tale which turned out to be true was of a tourist bus carrying Japanese tourists from Lima Airport to the centre of town. The bus had its tyres machine-gunned before the bandits robbed the tourists of their jewellery and other valuables, and all before they'd been in the country for five minutes.

The Peruvians I met were lovely people and it is a beautiful country. It is just unfortunate that at the end of the eighties the country was facing economic ruin and a small demographic of the pretty desperate population saw tourists as an easy target.

All I knew about Bolivia before I went was that La Paz popped up in Trivial Pursuit questions as the highest capital city in the world. That — and the fact its football team never seemed to qualify for the football World Cup finals. I'd agreed with the guide looking after my new-found friends, the spreaders of doom mentioned above, that I would accompany the small group, hitch a lift to the hydrofoil and cross the lake with them.

Lake Titicaca is beautiful and I found it hard to get my head around being in a boat some twelve thousand feet above sea level. That's only three thousand feet lower than Mont Blanc, the tallest mountain in the Alps. As we moored at the end of the journey we said our goodbyes, the tour picked up a bus and went on to La Paz. I walked a few yards to the Hotel Juatahata situated on the lake and a short distance from the town of Copacabana.

It was early afternoon. After checking in, I decided to visit the small man-made island a few hundred yards across the lake that I'd seen shortly before the hydrofoil docked. The local Indians had lived in these floating villages for centuries. It's thought by some that the Indians from Lake Titicaca were the first people to discover New Zealand and Australia. Thor Heyerdahl set out to prove this point when his Kon-Tiki expedition sailed across the Pacific in a boat of balsa wood and hemp back in 1947. Kon-Tiki was an Inca Sun God.

I drank tea, chatted to a couple of the islands' inhabitants and took my 'water taxi' back to the hotel. In my room I found a note from the manager inviting me to dinner. I was being terribly spoiled but I'd become used to this type of perk because hoteliers and airlines knew I was in the travel business and could turn out to be a possible source of revenue.

I met my host and after the obligatory questions about my nose I joined him in the small bar for a cocktail. My Spanish wasn't too bad in those days but Raul's English was perfect. The hotel was small and got most of its trade from passing traffic as tourists crossed the lake. It mainly provided lunches for the groups of tourists 'doing South America in ten days'. I asked how many guests were staying.

"Just you," he smiled. He told me he'd arranged an evening with local dancers and a guitarist. After an excellent meal and an enjoyable 'cultural feast' as he referred to it, I thanked Raul for his hospitality and made ready to retire.

"I must make a recommendation," said Raul with his hands clasped in a pleading gesture. "The sunrise over the lake is spectacular. Would you like me to arrange an early morning call?" I thanked him for the offer, accepted it and went to my room, feeling very chilly in the cold night mountain air as I scurried along the outside corridor overlooking the lake. When I entered the room, to my surprise, I found a large basket of strawberries alongside an ice bucket with a bottle of Chilean Champagne. Breakfast was sorted then.

I fell into bed and slept like a baby. It felt like the middle of the night when my wake-up call summoned me to life. It was still dark outside although I could just make out the very dim pre-light that signals the arriving dawn. I wrapped myself in the thick dressing-gown provided by the hotel and added my own quilted coat to protect me from the cold. I took the strawberries and the ice bucket out on to the balcony and settled back to witness Raul's 'spectacular'. I cracked open the bottle, took the cellophane wrapper off the basket of strawberries and settled down for breakfast.

The hotel was on stilts standing in the water on the edge of the lake. The lake is in the mountains with the mountain-top peaks looking like steep, pointed hills rather than mountains. As the sun crept up, it caught the blue of the lake and the white of the snow-covered mountains and the effect was breathtaking. The mountains were suddenly covered in pink icing sugar. I turned 360 degrees. For just a few minutes everything was the colour of a young girl's birthday cake. I wept with the beauty of it all and celebrated one of those all too rare sublime moments in life. Strawberries, champagne and a vision as beautiful as anything I've ever seen, before or since. As if it had been a dream, the sun continued its ascent and dawn turned to morning, leaving the pink vision as a beautiful memory. I didn't believe a 'Big Bang' could have created such beauty and it again made me wonder whether there was a God of Creation after all.

The stillness of it all brought back memories of the stand-off with the bully, Brian. This time it wasn't a stance and for the first time in my life I experienced a sense of connection with Creation.

I finished the strawberries and two-thirds of the champagne, showered, dressed and went to breakfast. A waiter was there to take my order. As I entered, he was straightening his bow-tie.

"Hey, amigo," said I in tipsy Spanish. I gestured for him to sit down with me and we polished off the rest of the champagne together.

I checked out of the hotel, left a note thanking Raul for his hospitality and hitched a lift in the hotel's laundry truck bound for La Paz, dozing off propped up against the laundry bags in the back of the vehicle. Raul will never fully know how much his kindness meant or how much of an impact his insistence that I witnessed the dawn had on me. Perhaps he was one more of the many angels who have watched over me on my journey.

My only recollection of the twenty-four-hour stay in La Paz was of walking up a long High Street, feeling as though I had a steel band around my chest. The effects of altitude made walking a real effort. I went on a short city tour and retired early to bed.

As I flew back to England the following day, I reflected on the paradox of love and hate which had embraced me during my South American adventure. Would I have enjoyed Machu Picchu, the beauty of the lake and the friendliness of the people in Peru and Bolivia as much without the violent mugging and the look of hatred on my assailants' faces? Would I have appreciated the kindness and generosity shown to me in Bolivia quite as much? Without the darkness of the night, would I have marvelled to the same extent at the beauty of the dawn on the lake? Had I not struggled for so long as a child, a boy, and then an adult, would I have found the experience of becoming the woman I was meant to be so incredibly liberating? On that flight home I realised I now had the strength to face up to my biggest challenge. I resolved to fix a firm date for my gender transition.

12

A TIME TO DO
OR A TIME TO DIE:
TRANSITION AND LOSS

"In the depth of winter I finally learned that there was within me an invincible summer."
Albert Camus

———————<>○<>———————

I was pretty certain South America would be my last overseas trip — at least for a while. It was time for my change of gender role and I knew I had to let my staff know. My Operations Manager, Anne, had asked me if I was ever going to have a haircut again. My weight loss from worry and not eating had drawn comments in the office.

Marie came in with me and we brought the staff into my office, two at a time, Noah's Ark-style and we told them what I was planning. Julie, one of the key members of staff, stopped me before I could say anything.

"I know what you're going to say," she exclaimed in a shrill voice.

"Go on," I said.

"You're changing sex."

"How did you guess?" I replied with surprise in my voice. I thought I'd hidden my plans pretty well.

Julie replied with a broad smile. "When we were horse riding in Arizona (we had been on a cowboy theme party on one of our travel programmes), I looked at you and thought, *I've never seen tits like that on a man before!*

Clearly the oestrogen had been working more effectively than I'd realised. At the end of the day only one employee handed in his notice. The following day I changed my name by statutory declaration and wrote to the DSS, HM Pensions, a host of insurance companies, banks and a plethora of institutions with a copy of my declaration authorised by a solicitor named Mr Dick. Nobody could make that up!

On Monday 11th February, six years after beginning hormone therapy, I placed all my male clothes in two black bin bags in the boot of my car for the charity shop. Everything except for a suit which Marie wanted as a keepsake. Looking back, I was very insensitive to her. This act symbolised the end of her husband. I didn't fully understand at the time just how painful that was for her and I should have done.

But for me it was the beginning of a new life. I donned my new business suit, a very smart navy blue Jacques Vert jacket and skirt topped off with a classic double-breasted raincoat and drove through thick snow to the office. After forty years I'd finally found the courage to change. Or rather, I'd become who I'd always felt *I was.* It was scary, yet totally liberating.

The word transsexual causes a lot of confusion because changing gender has nothing to do with sexuality; it has everything to do with a deep sense of *felt self.* On that February day I may have looked like a masculine woman and I still had bits of my still male body I desperately wanted to change but I was presenting myself to the world as the person I had always felt I really was. 'I' is a very difficult concept to explain to anyone who doesn't have a conflict between their mind and body. People have asked me why I chose to do what I did. I can only answer that *I* didn't choose *it. It* chose *me.* I didn't choose it any more than I chose my height or the natural colour of my hair.

My work colleagues were very accepting of their strange boss. The big question was 'What about the clients?' As a way of showing my appreciation to my staff at the office and as a bit of light relief, I paid for an outing to the Comedy Store in London. I sat in the fourth row praying nobody would pick on me. Frank Skinner, Bob Mills and Jo Brand were on the bill. Little did I know that one day I'd be standing on that very stage making people laugh.

A couple of weeks after my 'Big Day' my mother was taken into hospital for a minor operation to remove what she called 'my lump'. As I write this, I'm struck by how she took ownership of this foreign body rather than psychologically rejecting it. It is almost as though she let it in somehow. Mother was admitted to Ealing Hospital for what the doctor had described as a routine operation. Afterwards my father, Geraldine, Penny and I went to visit. Dad was distancing himself from me and Penny barely spoke. When we arrived, Mum was sitting up in bed looking very pleased with herself. "Look," she said. "They didn't have to remove it."

Geraldine and I looked at each other, confused. On the pretext of finding out when she could go home I went off to find her consultant. He wasn't around but after much stalling from the nursing staff, I tracked down his houseman.

"Can you tell me what's happening with Mrs Bridgman, please?" I asked.

"Sorry, who are you?" he replied.

"I'm her daughter," I said proudly.

"We decided not to remove her tumour," he continued.

We knew it was a tumour but this was the first time that I had heard the word used. The 'lump' morphed into something more sinister and the seriousness of her condition became embedded in my consciousness.

"Oh, so why didn't you remove it?" I asked him. The doctor explained that they had found a 'large mass' on her lungs. At this point I asked him to speak in English rather than using obtuse medical jargon in order to avoid what we both knew to be the reality. "Look, Doctor,

I'm not going to fall apart. Please tell me in plain English what the prognosis is."

He looked at me as if to say 'Are you sure?'

"Well, I'm not sure whether your mother should be told or not but she has a mass on both her lungs and they're too large to remove. We believe pain relief is the only way forward. I'm terribly sorry."

I thanked him, composed myself and returned to the ward with the intention of discussing it with my sisters later in the evening.

"So when can I go home?" my mother asked.

"Tomorrow," I replied, a manufactured smile on my face.

Later that evening my sisters and I decided to break the news to my father. Although my mother appeared to be in denial, she knew what was happening and she was dealing with it in her own way. She had a very deep faith which sustained her over the following weeks.

"You're killing your mother," said my father. "You're getting her stressed out and making her worse. Why don't you stay away?"

I was hurt but I knew he didn't mean it. He was angry with me and he was probably angry with God because he was losing his wife. So it was that in the early part of 1991 my mother's health quickly deteriorated and the health of my business Creative Destinations was declining just as alarmingly. I'd reckoned on losing some clients because of my big announcement but when our three major accounts after years of a great working relationship decided maybe it was a good time to change suppliers and go to our competitors, I knew we were in big trouble and would have to take drastic action. I was naive enough to think clients I'd known for years would be able to see beyond my transsexuality and continue their relationship with me, the person. I was sadly deluded.

I made the two BMW-driving account managers redundant. Deep down I knew it was too little too late. My new brother-in-law, Geraldine's husband Alan, stepped in to help with his financial background but we were on a steep downward spiral. From a turnover of well over a million in 1988 we'd gone down to a fraction of that figure which wouldn't even pay the overheads. We were sinking fast.

By late February Mum became very ill. She and I had many conversations when I visited her at home but my father didn't want me to visit in daylight in case the neighbours saw me. I exploded. "Look. Dad, the neighbours have gnomes fishing in the drains in their front garden and you're worried about what *they'll* think of *me*!"

Dad barely spoke to me and when he did, he insisted on calling me by my old male name. He was losing his wife and he had lost his son. That was how he saw it. I could understand this but it didn't make it any less painful. Mum was upset by what I'd done but more because she feared for me, Marie and the children. Her fears were not without foundation. I was deeply shocked by the rejection I was experiencing. Apart from my sister Penny and her family shunning me, several friends ceased contact. One of them said on the telephone via his wife, "I'd rather think of him as having died," to which I replied, "Well, tell him I'm f....ing alive," and hung up.

I suddenly felt very alone and isolated. My mother, my business and my friends were slipping away from me and I felt powerless to do anything about it.

By the middle of March Mum was unable to get out of bed unaided and the MacMillan cancer nurses made daily calls. With Dad in his mid-eighties my sisters and I operated a rota and slept on a small futon in my parents' flat so we were on hand to help Mum onto the commode when she needed it and help wash her and change bed linen. Her weight loss was staggering. This already thin woman had become skeletal. It was painful to witness her deterioration.

By the end of March the cancer had rendered her incapable of getting out of bed at all and the painkillers were failing to keep on top of the pain. In the first week of April she moved into the hospice attached to the Ealing Hospital. The night before she went in, she held my hand.

"I feel so ill. I don't want to feel ill anymore."

She'd had enough. She was ready to die. She gave up the fight around the fifth of April and slipped into a coma. Our conversation on the eve of her admission to the hospice was the last lucid interaction I had with her.

We kept up a round-the-clock vigil, not knowing how long she'd last. One of the nurses suggested my father get some sleep every night because we were all worried about his health. My sisters and I worked out a nighttime rota so one of us would be there with her all the time. The night of the 10th April was my 'shift'.

I slept on a camp bed next to her bed with the head just beyond the foot of her bed. That way I could see her at all times, propped up with pillows without having to move and disturb her. I settled down to read, frequently glancing at her face to see if there was any expression in her eyes. Her breathing had a chesty rattle. It was disconcerting to see her eyes. They were in a permanent state of semi-closure with half-hooded lids. There was no light in them. It was almost as though she had already left her body.

At around two a.m. I glanced up and noticed something was different. Although she appeared to be sleeping, there was life in her eyes. I stared at her for a few moments.

"You know I'm here, don't you?" I said softly. There was the minutest flicker of an eyelid as if to acknowledge my enquiry. I picked up a prayer book from her bedside table and sat on the edge of the bed to read to her. I took her skeletal hand in mine and began reading. The prayer I chose had a line in it describing death.

"When my ship comes to take me home, may the pilot be the Christ God." As I read the words, her fingers tightened very slightly around mine. In a coma she could still communicate. I read for a few more minutes and after kissing her forehead I returned to my bed to try and grab a few minutes sleep.

Less than a minute later there was a change to her breathing. The rhythm had become erratic and the in-breaths were longer and laboured, as though she was struggling to breathe. I called the nurse who came in, took her pulse and looked at me. "I think you'd better call your father," she said. I went to the phone on the neighbouring nurse's station and called home.

"Dina, you need to bring Dad. Mum's going."

As I put the phone down, I heard a gasp and a long rattle. I walked into the room and the nurse looked up at me and told me what I already knew. I don't think I cried. I just walked over and stroked her hair back, kissed her on the forehead again and said goodbye. The nurse invited me to help straighten her out so she would look nice for Dad. I combed her hair, put her dentures in her mouth and placed her hands on her chest holding a small framed photograph of her babies, my three sisters and I.

Twenty minutes later footsteps in the corridor announced the arrival of my father, sisters and Penny's daughter, my niece Caroline. They walked into the room and Penny burst into tears.

My father said, "How is it they can put a man on the moon but they can't cure cancer?" His question sounded childlike but it was his way of asking, 'Why did she have to go?'

At the foot of the bed I saw my father weep for only the second time in my life. My sisters and Caroline joined him, forming a circle with their arms around each other's shoulders, united in grief. I went to join them but as I tried to put my arms around their shoulders, my father pulled his elbow back to shrug me away. I retreated until I felt the wall at my back. Seeing my anguish the nurse came over, put her arms around me and hugged me. It was the first time an adult had physically hugged me since my transition.

An hour or so later I drove through the morning half-light just prior to sunrise back to my father's flat in Northolt. I offered to sort out the death certificate and to pick up Mum's clothes from the hospital. Within about two hours of leaving the hospice, I was driving back. I picked up the ubiquitous black dustbin sack containing her belongings and returned to the room where she'd died. I needed to pick up the photo frame she'd clutched in death. But more than that, I wanted to feel her spirit had left. The room confirmed she was gone. It is a feeling that is hard to articulate but I felt an empty coldness which had replaced her warmth and humanity.

My mother bequeathed me a beautiful gift. She chose to die when I was present and she showed me how to die with dignity. Not for her the pleading for life or bargaining for more time with her Maker, just a wish to go home. Clearly she couldn't have chosen to live for another three months but I do believe we can make a choice. Elephants go home to die and humans too get a choice, albeit a limited one. It was terribly sad but it was also one of the richest experiences of my life. My mother gave me life and she showed me how to let go of it when the time came.

A couple of days later my sisters came round to discuss the funeral arrangements. They told me my father wanted me to attend the funeral as his 'son'. If I insisted on wearing female clothes, he didn't want me there. I'd been half-expecting it but I was still disappointed and hurt. I said I couldn't possibly do it. I didn't have any male clothes anymore and anyway I wouldn't subject myself to that.

"Why shouldn't I be who I am?" I asked them angrily.

Penny gave me a dismissive wave of the hand.

"Well, you know Mum hated all this." There was bile in her voice.

To my shame, I eventually agreed that I wouldn't travel with the family in the funeral procession. I skulked like a criminal into the back of the church. I stood with the family that mattered and held the hands of my two wonderful children, with my amazing partner Marie at my side.

At the crematorium the vicar asked Dad where his son was. Dad told him I was abroad on business. As far as my relatives were concerned, I just wasn't present. After the service Marie, the girls and I left without speaking to anyone in the family. A few hours later my nephew Robert and his wife called round to see if we were ok. Apparently everyone else had gone back to my parent's flat for a mini-wake, drinks and nibbles. Clearly I was an embarrassment and was not invited. This final act of denial made my anger rise up within me. That evening through a haze of alcohol I wrote a long letter to my sister Penny, expressing my hurt and disgust over the way I'd been treated.

"Is what I've become so awful?" I wrote. "How dare you not want me near at the funeral?" My anger and my tears poured out onto the keyboard. It probably wasn't the best way to respond but I could no longer rein in my emotions.

About two weeks later Penny wrote back. 'I'm sorry you're so bitter, but what did you expect?'

I've seen her twice since my mother's death and then only at my father's and my sister Geraldine's funerals. I've tried and continue to keep the door open for future contact. Looking back, I realise that whatever happened on that truly dreadful day, nobody could take away the rich experience of my mother's passing. Nobody could take away the fact that she chose to share her death with me. That experience we shared and her memory have sustained me ever since.

CONVERSATION WITH OSCAR WILDE

"Always forgive your enemies; nothing annoys them so much."
Oscar Wilde

When I look at this phase of my life it is as though I had it all. But to be who I am, I had to risk everything. There are two writers who share the top spot in my affection and admiration. Charles Dickens is one writer who has an unparalleled ability to paint pictures with words. The other is Oscar Wilde who had the gift to write about almost anything with intelligence and rapier-like wit. He must rank as one of the greatest writers of his or any generation. I wondered what he would make of change and living his truth if I were able to speak with him.

Mr Wilde, what were you feeling when your need for love took you into a place that had the potential to destroy you?

I think everyone makes that mistake.

What mistake?

My dear, it wasn't my need for love, it was my need to be true to myself. I'd become the world's greatest social butterfly but it was all a pretence. Sycophantic socialites hung on my every word as though my utterings were of genius. I was a genius of course, but I was merely expressing my boredom with their tedious questions. I married a lovely woman and had beautiful children, but I was living a lie.

So why did you put yourself in a position where you'd be attacked and vilified?

Initially, like you I was petrified of what society would do to me. The enormity of my position would mean a spectacular fall from grace. In Victorian Britain sexuality wasn't openly discussed, just as in twentieth century Britain gender identity was a taboo subject. Well, except in ghastly television programmes. My life was in danger of becoming a parody of the very things I despised in the society in which I moved.

There was a disregard for people who didn't fit in with society. Hypocrisy was a cancer in that world. I reached a point where the cost of living a lie was just too much.

Did you ever regret it?

I have to admit there were times in prison where I wondered what on earth I'd done but through that pain came some of my best work.

Talking of which, whenever I read your books, I want to cry.

Surely they aren't that bad?

No, The Little Prince *is quite simply the most exquisite story of unrequited love ever told. I totally identified with all of the 'beings' in that story.*

You're not going sycophantic on me, are you?

No. I really mean it. The reason I asked to speak with you was because your wonderful prose kept me going in my darkest hour. Even your most frivolous plays had meaning and depth. The Importance of Being Earnest *was such a great parody of family life.*

I am glad you enjoyed it. I'd hate to be remembered for one elderly actress uttering, "A haaaaand baaaag," although I have to say I loved Dame Edith Evans. But my dear child, these frivolous plays as you call them were the only things that really mattered. Remember, I was first and foremost a playwright, an entertainer. I used humour to get my views across. I wanted to show society up for what it was; class-ridden and ruled by people who didn't have to work for a living. I had a wonderful time but I was always an outsider who was tolerated as long as I entertained. The job of an artist or entertainer is to speak truthfully about the unspeakable. When you can do that in your comedy, you'll be a great success as an artist and as a member of the human race.

When I first read The History of Man Under Socialism, *I was amazed by the content. It was years ahead of its time. What moved you to write it?*

As I said, I was an outsider. I was tolerated because I could amuse and I was able to write. I knew they'd hate me if they really knew me and so I wore a mask of acceptability. Deep down I was a man of the people and the 'proletariat' existed to feed the society in which I moved. God gifted me the ability to write and I wrote for my supper. When I could, I commented on something meaningful. I may have moved in high society, but deep down I was a man of the people. Look, what you have to remember is when you're different and you challenge the norm, people look at you and they see part of themselves. In you they see the side of themselves they cannot face. They see a dark corner of their own minds and it scares them. It scares them so much they attack you, as though by attacking you they can rid themselves of their own demons. I fell in love with someone who was dangerous and unobtainable and I knew what I was risking, but not to do it was risking everything. I was risking a life of denial and fear. Not to have done it would have been to die.

You once said you were going to commit a great folly. Do you still see it as that?

Of course, but as I illustrated in my plays, folly is the only truth. Following the rules is a lie because they're not *your* rules. They're not rules born from love and are not *of* you. For me to perpetuate the lie would have been a far greater folly, for it would have been a denial of myself and I would have been far more dishonest than my persecutors.

When I read The Ballad of Reading Gaol, *I wept buckets. I somehow sat with you in your cell and understood what being different meant for the first time. The brave man killing with a sword and the coward with a kiss is possibly the greatest truth ever written. Your work somehow sustained me through my teens and into my adulthood.*

Well, of course it did because your truth is your truth and nobody else's truth. It is the only thing that matters. We all avoid pain and we mistakenly believe that by avoiding change we're avoiding pain. The point is, of course, that we are not changing ourselves, we are merely facing up to who we really are. We may change our appearance, we may even change our bodies but we cannot, nor should we try to, change who we are. If we're good enough for God, we should be good enough for mere humanity. Remember we can only come back home to who we are, who we are in all our magnificence and with all our wonderful frailties. Not that I had any of course!!

Thank you for spending this short time with me, I may come back again if that's OK?

Of course but before you go, tell me something. What did you discover that being different meant?

I learned that being different isn't about being different at all, it just means being myself.

It takes a few seconds to say it, but it's taken me years of struggle to understand it.

12
ONE STEP AT A TIME

"You take a little seed, plant it, water it, and fertilize it for a whole year, and nothing happens. The second year you water it and fertilize it, and nothing happens. The third and fourth year you water it and fertilize it, and nothing happens. How discouraging this becomes! The fifth year you continue to water and fertilize the seed and then---take note. Sometime during the fifth year, the Chinese bamboo tree sprouts and grows NINETY FEET IN SIX WEEKS."
The growth process of the Chinese Bamboo tree
as told by Zig Ziglar

———◦◦———

My change of gender caused a much bigger stir than I'd imagined it would. I really didn't foresee the extent of rejection I'd encounter. One by one I wrote to people I thought of as friends. Many of them just didn't like the idea of associating with a transsexual. I knew transsexuals had a bad press but I discovered that for a lot of people it's just too scary.

What I looked like mattered a great deal. I didn't look like Claudia Schiffer and I had a deep voice. 'Welcome to our world!' is what I imagine most women on the planet might say to that injustice.

Even driving a car became a very different experience. I found myself subjected to verbal abuse from drivers to a degree I'd never experienced before. A polite wave of the hand to let me into traffic on a main road happened less frequently. Maybe it was me being more sensitive to it. Or perhaps it was my poor driving.

It wasn't all bad. I noticed that other women became more communicative with me. Conversations at supermarket checkouts or in shops would strike up and friendly pleasantries would be exchanged, whereas before everything seemed more formal.

The first time I went for a night out with a bunch of girls it was brilliant. I hadn't laughed so much in years. Most of the group ordered pints of lager while I ordered a glass of wine. So much for gender stereotypes!

My company, Creative Destinations, was in trouble before the end of 1990 but after my transition and the loss of our major clients, it became terminally ill. Consultants told me to scale right back and sell the business as a going concern. But I'm bloody-minded. Determined not to fail I dug in, refused to accept defeat and looked for new clients. With the glorious benefit of hindsight I should have sold the business and moved on before my transition. I had become too absorbed in my own problems and hadn't paid enough heed to the warning signs of economic recession. Companies were cutting back on expenditure and overseas incentive travel trips were no longer a priority.

Eventually there wasn't enough money to pay the staff their salaries so I paid them from my credit card. Juggling bills had sadly become the main part of my job. The Operations Manager told me the staff were worried. I said there was no need but I must have lacked conviction. We soldiered on and I continued paying the staff their salaries from my credit cards. By now I was £305,000 in debt, including the personal guarantees I'd given the bank. In 1991 that was an awful lot of money.

I came to terms with the inescapable fact that we had nowhere to go. However optimistic I tried to be with the numbers, the truth was that we were insolvent. I broke the news to Marie. She was worried but as always, she supported me. On Monday I called in the accountants and I received what I now know to be very poor advice. They told me to place the limited company into voluntary liquidation. They arranged a clearing house to remove all the office equipment and sell it for me and that clearing house kept ninety per cent of the value of the goods, my business receiving about ten per cent. What I should have done was sold the assets and put the funds in the bank account before placing the company into the hands of the Receiver. That piece of bad advice cost me about £30,000. I was too naive and, dare I say, honest.

It may have changed since the late eighties but the people working at the so-called business bank had no experience of business and no knowledge of business affairs. They were worse than useless when I needed them most. But good advice or bad, I have to put my hands up and admit it was me who lost control because I was so sidetracked by my personal issues. I got it wrong and I paid the price. But actually my business failure and my change of gender were to herald in a new life. They were the making of me. But before I could move forward, I had to deal with my debts. Like most people who go into business with little experience and minimal financial backing, I donned the mythical protection of a limited company and in exchange was forced to sign a personal guarantee to obtain credit. Now it was payback time and the bank wanted their money.

My employees accused me of salting away money and causing them to miss out financially when the company closed down. It was very hurtful, particularly as I'd paid the salaries from my personal bank account. Just to rub salt in the wound, the bank refused to cease adding interest on the company debt. As everyone knows, banks never lose out to their customers. On the day of the bankruptcy hearing I drove to London to face the abuse of the creditors who'd turned up to see what they might get. I came out of the hearing to find I had a parking ticket. I guess when your luck runs out, it really does run out.

So in five months, I'd changed my gender, lost my mother and liquidated my business with massive personal debts and little prospect of employment. To call it an eventful time would be like calling the Second World War a minor skirmish!

I signed on at the dole queue for the first time in my life. They asked me all the usual questions and I had to explain my change of name to bemused interviewers. I'm very proud of the fact that despite everything that had happened I was only unemployed for two months. Well, you can't keep a good woman down!

What to do? I couldn't stay in the travel business. Prior to my change of gender the phone rang every week as I was headhunted by someone or other. But post gender transition I had become a leper and the phone stopped ringing.

Headlines in the trade press didn't help. 'Sex Change causes the Demise of Leading Incentive Travel House,' read one of the more absurd headlines. Not an accurate statement on many levels. At that point I had changed my gender *role* but had not yet had my much wanted sex reassignment surgery. I had more pressing needs. Operations felt way, way for the future. I was in the midst of a survival battle.

A chance conversation helped shape the direction of my career. The person who sold me a Group Pension Plan for my employees came to see me. She suggested I consider a career in financial services. Her words struck a chord with me. "If you're prepared to work hard, you'll earn a good living." Here was an opportunity for me to start a new career as a woman, with no need to explain my past.

One interview seemed to go quite well and I was called back for a second and then a third interview. At the third interview I wondered if they suspected something and whether I'd carried off my transition very well. I took the bull by the horns.

"Look, Mr P, this is my third interview and I'm guessing you're worried about something."

He looked at me. "Since you've brought it up, there is."

I waited for the question. "We're worried you won't be able to put the time in because of your two children."

Wow. So there I was being treated like any other woman and experiencing the prejudices every woman encounters. Marie joked that I was paying my dues.

"Oh, don't worry," I told them. "I'm totally committed."

Eventually I was taken on as a trainee Sales Associate by Allied Dunbar, a company with a reputation for excellent training. Armed with a ton of study material I went on holiday to Cornwall in a friend's holiday cottage with Marie and the girls. I didn't even know what an endowment policy was, but I was about to find out.

I did my induction training in Swindon, came out second from top in my intake and headed off to begin a career as a non-salaried, commission-only Sales Associate, determined to succeed. Life was looking up again. But there was still the matter of that bank debt.

It was my first day working as a woman in a newly qualified, no salary, commission role as a Financial Adviser. I was nervous but excited by the opportunity to take control of my life again. I was allotted a desk and joined a meeting for me and the three other new recruits, all of whom were men. Sean, the trainer, was in full motivational flow.

"Right, you lot, time to work your balls off." He stopped and glanced at me.

"Sorry. I didn't mean you, Michelle."

Well, that would save me £6,000, I thought to myself. £6,000 was the going rate for sex reassignment surgery at the time. Inwardly, I was beaming. He'd taken me for a woman. Right now that was all I wanted. Well, that and an income.

It was time for another bank meeting. The last time the bank manager had seen me I was wearing a man's suit and tie with trousers. Turning up in a Jacques Vert skirt and jacket, court shoes and makeup probably didn't inspire him with confidence. After polite negotiations he said he was sorry but the bank needed their money within ninety days or it would take action to get it. *It* meant losing the house.

Dejected, I left the office. As I walked out onto the street, I snapped. Sod them, I thought. I am *not* losing my home. I went home, drew up a plan and drove back to the bank that same afternoon. I sailed past reception with the receptionist vainly trying to stop me and marched back into the manager's office. He was in a meeting with a colleague. I slammed my fist on the table and spilled his coffee everywhere.

"You're *not* taking my house. I've got a concrete plan."

I left thirty minutes later having reduced the debt to £120,000 so long as I repaid it within a month. I remortgaged our house and set about earning an income. The experience with the bank taught me four things:

You have more power than you think with creditors

By taking action, anything's possible

You need belief in yourself to make it happen

You must have absolute determination

Allied Dunbar was very good at incentivising the Sales Associates. I went from zero to hero and ended my first year as the top rookie in the branch. Awards followed and I enjoyed slap-up lunches at restaurants like the famous Michel Roux's Waterside Inn in Bray and Le Manoir aux Quat'saisons, owned by the amazing chef, Raymond Blanc.

Earning a living as a Financial Advisor was never my goal in life, but it afforded me the opportunity to get back on my feet and grow. I gained the strength to fight the National Health Service who refused to fund my surgery because it was 'non-essential'. My Member of Parliament and I fought to get NHS funding which was not always available at the time. He supported my case and unblocked the funding jam.

13
BODY OF TRUTH

"Better a diamond with a flaw than a pebble without."
Confucius

———◦———

I had my surgery on 1st November 1995, six years after changing my gender role and nine years after beginning hormone therapy. I chose November as I needed two months recuperation time and December was a quiet month in financial services.

I checked into the London Bridge Hospital the day before on 31st October for routine X-rays and a horrible colonic irrigation to reduce the risk of infection in the surgical area. I then began eight days of nil by mouth, a drastic but effective method of detoxing!

My surgeon, the lovely Mr D, dropped in to see if I had any questions and I was asked to sign a disclaimer. He seemed to be ensuring that he couldn't be sued if I claimed afterwards that it was a mistake.

During the afternoon the Chaplain from neighbouring Guy's Hospital came in and we had a brief chat.

"What are you having done?" he enquired.

"Sex-reassignment surgery," was my reply, expecting him to run out of the door.

He hesitated for a moment. "Do you mind me asking which way you are going?"

I held back a laugh and mischievously responded with a flirtatious, "Which way would you prefer?"

After a brief pause he broke into laughter and shared the joke with me.

Later in the evening, the psychiatrist called in. David was the brother of the surgeon so it appeared to be something of a family business.

"Michelle," he said. "I have to ask you one last time, 'Have you changed your mind?'"

"No, David, I still don't fancy you," was my reply.

"I think you're ready," David said with a smile on his face and left the room.

That night I slept soundly and was woken early for my pre-med jab and the journey down to theatre. A smiling surgeon gave me a reassuring smile and I drifted off for a long sleep.

I awoke in the recovery room around noon after the four-hour operation and drifted off to sleep again to be awoken by a throbbing sensation in the lower half of my body. I was on a morphine drip but could still feel a heavy ache, although everything was numb from the epidural which was administered just prior to surgery to ensure that all the muscles were relaxed.

After the surgery to construct my new vagina from my old male anatomy, everything was held in with a huge wad of dressing for seven days. A catheter was in place to expel the many litres of water I was asked to drink every day.

During the first night I struggled with the pain and they injected me with Pethidine painkillers to supplement the morphine drip. After twenty-four hours I was sitting up in bed enjoying a bit of banter with the nurse. I felt euphoric. The long years of waiting were finally over.

Marie came to visit with a friend. It was good to see her but I was aware it must have been a very difficult visit as her husband had now finally made the irreversible bodily changes. Until now those changes had been a concept, a thing of the future.

On the seventh day the surgeon arrived to remove the packing that was keeping everything in place, along with dozens of stitches. Next came the catheter and I was ready for my first proper pee. He warned me the swelling might prevent me from peeing naturally and that the catheter might need to be replaced for a further couple of days.

But a couple of hours later I lurched, weak from lack of food, to the bathroom. I sat down and after a moment there was a 'whoosh'. To my relief it worked perfectly. I cried, "Yes, yes!!" and burst into tears. The nurse came running in.

"What's wrong?"

I yelled, "I can pee properly."

"Oh!" she said, leaving the room with an 'is that all?' air.

That was it. Quite simply, for the first time in my life I could go to the bathroom and function in a manner that to me was normal. Having sex reassignment surgery was a great relief after all the years working towards aligning my body with my mind. It had nothing to do with sex. What it meant to me was that I could at last look in the mirror and see an image that didn't distress me. I could go to public toilets without doing a double take on the door lock to make sure nobody could burst in. I could use changing rooms to try on clothes in fashion shops without fear of exposure. In short, for the first time in my life I felt normal.

It's very hard to explain all the things I felt post-surgery. In essence nothing much had changed. Nobody knew what was under my clothes, but I did. It was as though the black and white movie I'd been watching was now in glorious technicolour and rather than watching it, I was now starring in it. I felt unstoppable.

I even survived an attempt at blackmail some months later when someone thought they could get me to part with money in return for their silence. When I wouldn't play ball, they wrote to my employers wrongly accusing me of mis-selling.

I was now 'outed' at work but at least now there were no secrets. After an investigation I was cleared and resumed my career. But I was becoming increasingly frustrated by only having one company's products to sell. I knew there was more to my career than selling financial products. The way I saw it, I had changed my gender, how difficult would it be to change business identities, yet again? I became an Independent Financial Advisor (IFA) but it was really financial services that I had tired of and it wasn't long before I was seeking an exit from the profession. I decided to sell my financial practice.

Alongside working in the financial sector I'd become more and more interested in counselling but it had been my experience as a Samaritan volunteer that had really fuelled my interest. The truth is that I never felt working in finance to be a calling and wanted something more.

Fifteen years earlier, back in 1975 it was the loneliness of holding my dreaded secret that encouraged me to volunteer with the Samaritans. It would be nice to say I volunteered out of a sense of pure altruism but the truth is I hoped supporting people who were desperate or lonely might alleviate my own isolation.

I still think listening to someone on the phone is the best basic training for anyone who is intent on really listening to another person. Volunteers were only asked to do four or five three-hour shifts in a six week rota, one of those being a night shift. Night shifts were always fun. There were sometimes long silent periods when the phone wouldn't ring and we'd get some sleep or exchange anecdotes from our camp beds. On other occasions the calls went non-stop through the night.

The job was a great leveller. About every six years I'd be scheduled to do a night shift on Christmas Eve. On one such occasion I was feeling rather smug about being such a generous soul, giving up my time on Christmas Eve. I took a call from a woman who had recently separated from her husband and was spending her first Christmas alone with two young children.

After about half an hour she suddenly asked, "How old are you?"

"Twenty-seven," I replied.

"Then what the f.... can you know about life?" She hung up the phone. Perhaps I wasn't such a hero after all!

During my tenure at the Chiltern branch of the Samaritans I supervised shifts, trained new and existing volunteers and ran workshops at the annual conference in York. It all proved to be a great grounding. The work of a Samaritan volunteer is hugely valuable and after about fifteen years as a volunteer, I was more and more drawn to taking it further. I wanted to do face-to-face work and researched career options in Counselling and Psychotherapy. I decided to try and qualify as a Counsellor and enrolled on a three-year part-time Counselling course at Southwark College.

It was 1989 and by this time I was taking hormones. Although I had made the decision to change my gender role, no date had been fixed. I'd be living in the female role at some point and so I explained the position to the course administrators and enrolled as Michelle. Because I was still mainly living and working in the male role it meant every Monday afternoon I'd change, get in the car inside the garage so the neighbours didn't see me, then accelerate quickly down the road and set off on my journey to Peckham, South London for the course.

The counselling course was self-facilitated, which meant that although we had tutors, we made our own decisions within the parameters of the course and our learning agreements. It was a diverse group of twenty-five people of varying cultures, sexualities and ethnic backgrounds. Oh, and of course me. It was the first time I'd encountered the politics of race, sexuality and religion all in one room. As part of the counselling course we sampled some of the different orientations used in psychotherapy. Psychotherapy is perhaps best defined as a more interactive form of counselling, although one or two genres are still very much based on listening and reflecting back to the client.

I was attracted to Gestalt, a style of therapy largely devised by Fritz Perls and Paul Goodman. Roughly translated, Gestalt means completion. The immediacy of interaction in the present, the 'Here and Now' made a lot of sense to me. It's a very different approach to the more traditional analytical approaches. I enrolled on the Diploma Course at the Metanoia Institute with the option to extend it to a master's degree at Middlesex University. Yet again, the irony of the university name didn't escape me!

The course was demanding but richly rewarding. It was a very proud day when I graduated from my Master's Degree and was photographed in my blue gown with Marie and the girls beside me. It had taken forty years since leaving school at fifteen but I'd made it. Perhaps I wasn't stupid after all.

Some days after the event I realised the University Chancellor who presented me with my degree was the former C.E.O. of one of the Grand Metropolitan group of companies I'd escorted on a trip to Hamburg. Doubtless he failed to make a connection between the tall woman receiving her Masters and the skinny guy who took him on an incentive trip.

A chance meeting at the graduation ceremony party resulted in me taking my education further. A professor engaged me in conversation and I was intrigued by his East London twang. My stereotypical view of an academic was of someone in a cardigan with a plummy Oxbridge accent who'd just stepped off the set of an Inspector Morse episode. This friendly don asked me the obvious question, "What next?"

I told him I'd been approached to write a book with a professor at a well-known London Institute. It was a manual for psychotherapists working in the field of gender identity disorders. He asked me if there would be a lot of research involved and wondered if I'd considered doing a doctorate.

"Oh, I couldn't do that," said I. "I'm not an academic."

"You've just got a Master's degree!" He pushed his face close to mine and looked me right in the eye. "******g get over it and do the Doctorate."

The idea of contributing to the field of psychotherapy grew on me. Two weeks and three interviews later I enrolled on the course at the same Middlesex University. My foray into the deeper world of academia was under way.

My inquisitiveness about what makes us function had its earliest stirrings from the moment I realised I was different. I've always had a fascination with the human condition and psychology. Studying psychotherapy became something of an obsession. Walk into any bookshop and you'll find thousands of titles in the Mind and Spirit section from *How To Become Successful in 7 days* to *I Can Change Your Life*. It's always fascinated me the way the personal development industry and the people selling products in that field have polarised with the world of psychotherapy. Self-help gurus tend to use Neuro-Linguistic Programming (NLP) and accuse psychotherapy of taking forever to achieve anything and the psychotherapy world is wary of practices like NLP, which they suspect will only offer temporary respite from neuroses and life's ills.

We live in a microwave age where people want instant fulfilment but they're not always prepared to look deep enough within themselves to find the answers. They trudge from seminar to seminar looking for the elixir that will put everything right *for* them.

To suggest all psychotherapy is worthless or that every self-help programme is 'snake oil' would be a misrepresentation, but the user should check out extravagant claims and speak with former participants of any such programme before parting with hard earned cash.

I've studied dozens of methods and attended countless seminars and study events in my pursuit of contentment and fulfilment as well as knowledge. I have an MSc in Gestalt Psychotherapy and I'm an NLP Master Practitioner. So which method is the best? I think it depends more on how they are applied but when I work, I respect the fact that each client is unique. There cannot be a 'one size fits all' approach. Different methods work for different people and they are all part of a learning process, not a magic wand. I have to use all the tools in my toolbox as and when they are needed.

Many people struggle to attain fulfilment and success because they can't define what those things really mean or they are trying to be something or someone they are not. True happiness comes when you finally accept who you are *but* accepting who you are only happens when you go on your own personal journey of exploration. The length of or how long your journey takes depends on how many barriers you place in your path to avoid really looking at yourself. And the distractions you construct to sabotage your own journey correlate to how badly you wish to avoid who you are meant to be.

In the end, you're not alone. The unconditional love and support of family and friends assisted me more than I can say. I've talked about meeting Marie and having two children but only in the context of what was going on for me at the time of the upheaval. The simple fact is, having a loving family has been the most important, most incredible experience of my life. Without them I would have no story to tell. Without them and their uncompromising love, it's absolutely certain I would not have survived.

When Marie and I met we had no idea we were entering into a relationship that would last for forty years and maybe more. Nor did we envisage the relationship having to cope with the massive changes that were to ensue. Marie's willingness to adjust and adapt to a very different life to the one she had envisaged took remarkable courage and great strength of character.

Through everything she held the family together, brought up two daughters and supported me through my highs and lows. How did she cope with everything that was going on in our lives during those mad years when I was flying around the world in an alcoholic haze and physically changing before her very eyes? The answer is, I honestly don't know. What I *do* know is she was prepared to let love dictate her decisions.

I can think of no better illustration of unconditional love. Her love for me was bolstered by her compassion. She could see the person she loved going through a traumatic experience and she loved me enough to set aside her fear of losing me. When I finally owned up to what was happening with me, if you'd asked her whether we'd be together for another thirty years, she'd have probably struggled to commit to thirty days. But we took one day at a time.

I always made it clear that whatever happened to me or to our relationship, I'd always do whatever it took to bring up the children to the best of my ability. I did my best but the truth is Marie was the parent who was always there for them, particularly when I was working around the clock to secure our financial survival.

In the years before my transition I was either genuinely working late, or abroad and out in clubs leading a double life, while Marie assumed I was working. Did she know what I was up to? I hid it well and I lived a very schizophrenic existence. It was the businessman and the father giving way to the part of me that yearned to express herself, albeit in a twilight world at the time.

Because the children were the glue that held us together, I regret that I cut such an unconventional father figure but I knew we all loved each other. I was imperfect but I was determined to do my best. Marie was the person who liaised with the school and made sure the girls were ok. We agreed I would stay out of the picture for the sake of the children at school. That meant she was the only parent at open days, sports days or for the school play.

Marie has incredible emotional strength. Coping with me and bringing up the children were enough on their own but she also had to cope with being shunned by neighbours and a few so-called friends. She tired of the insensitive and almost inevitable questions.

"Why did you stay?"

"What's in it for you?"

"Are you a lesbian?"

The crassness of some of the comments was mind-boggling. People just couldn't seem to understand we were together because, in spite of my change of gender, I still loved Marie and despite the fact she had lost her husband, she still loved me.

Even after some of those people came to accept her decision to stay, they didn't understand that she had to go through a grieving process. Although we stayed together, she'd still lost her husband and Marie was grieving. When we lost the business and were worried about our finances and losing the house, she always trusted me to pull through. When I borrowed money or ran up credit card debt, she trusted my judgment and my ability to put food on the table. She never lost faith in me and I will never forget that. I owe her everything.

Marie is also a wonderful mother. The fact that Laura and Susie turned out to be such amazing young women is down in no small part to the fantastic parenting job that she did. When we discovered that they suffered from dyslexia, it was Marie who fought for support from clinicians and teachers until she was heard. As the children grew up, Marie went back to work and trained as a schoolteacher so she could supplement the household income. When she was diagnosed with lupus, a chronic illness, she still put the needs of the family first and carried on working.

The children were a great motivation for us to keep together as a family but it doesn't explain why we are still together now. It would be easy to say it's because we love each other. That's true but quite simply we realised that we were and still are best friends. We've both paid a price. The reaction of others is one thing. Neither of us wanted a physical relationship with the other and so we set aside the need for a sexual relationship in order to maintain our marriage.

Growing up with a transsexual father was not the easiest path for my daughters. We were fortunate they were in a good school at the time of my transition but children can be cruel with barbed taunts and teasing. The teachers were very supportive and the Head Teacher ensured her teaching staff kept an eye open for any negative behaviour from the other girls.

When they were older, I asked them, "Were you bullied?"

"Look, we dealt with it," they replied. "OK?"

On one of my early excursions 'out' to the Natural History Museum in London, I stepped out of the car nervously in my smart two-piece outfit. Laura was just seven or eight years old. She took my hand reassuringly.

"I'll look after you."

I was warmed by her response but guilty and ashamed that my daughter was put in that position.

Growing into adulthood the girls continued to display sensitivity and love. Both have been unafraid to tell friends and boyfriends about their 'father'. On the eve of meeting Laura's partner for the first time I asked her what she'd told him about me. (I always told them I didn't mind what they chose to say because I knew it would vary according to who they met.)

"Oh, I told him exactly what the position is," she said. "I think their response provides a good judge of character."

IMAGINARY CONVERSATION WITH SOJOURNER TRUTH

"Truth is powerful and it prevails."
Sojourner Truth

The period following my change of gender and the loss of my business was a rebuilding phase. I had to start a new career, rebuild my finances and find my place as a woman in the world. This last one was the easy part because I only had to allow myself to be who I'd always felt I was. The thing was, a lot of people in my world found me a problem. I left an industry I loved to work in the finance industry. That career didn't come naturally to me but did at least provide me with a launchpad for my new life.

To reflect on this phase of my life and what it meant, I spoke to another of my sheroes and imagined what she'd say. There's very little on record in respect of this extraordinary woman who lived before the days of newsreels. But one single speech gave her a place in American folklore. She is an inspiration to not only African Americans, but to women everywhere.

Isabella Baumfree was born into slavery in New York State in 1797. She inherited the name given to her by her Dutch owners but after a religious conversion in 1843 she took the name Sojourner Truth, which translated means 'Travelling Preacher'.

Her most famous speech, *Ain't I A Woman?*, was delivered in 1851 at a Women's Rights Convention in Ohio. In it she eloquently argued for the rights of women using the analogy of Christ being born of a woman and of God with no man involved. Forcibly arguing, "Ain't I a woman?" She travelled widely and despite her lack of a formal education, spoke passionately and forcefully for African Americans and for women's rights. She fought alongside Lincoln's administration and she was a force behind the Emancipation Movement in America.

To live as a woman was a struggle for me and it took all my fortitude. But of course living as a woman is still a struggle for many women around the world. Sojourner Truth overcame extraordinary odds and

I can think of nobody braver or more suitable to be one of my sheroes and for me to consult than her.

When I first read about you I was somewhat daunted by the formidable person you are. You had enormous strength of character.

Only somewhat daunted? What does that mean? Either you is or you ain't?

OK, I was daunted.

That's better. You and me gonna get on fine if you speak plain truth and say what you mean.

I've just been talking about a period of my life where I had to change direction and dig in to survive. Your whole life was spent 'digging in'. How did you find the strength?

You don't find it. *It* is there already. God put it there. You just have to tap into it. Our own experience is the only one we know. To you, what I lived through as a slave was unimaginable but what you lived through is beyond comprehension to me. The Lord delivers us a hand and we have to get on with it. It ain't easy but with his help, anything is possible.

While you were working for one particular family, you discovered your previous 'owner' sold one of your sons to a slave owner in Alabama. You went to court and successfully argued he was emancipated under New York law and you won him back. How did you find the resources to do that?

There ain't no love like the love a mother has for her children. That's for starters. And I may have been born into slavery but the Good Lord didn't make me no slave. My spirit was always free and my spirit was good and strong. I determined I would win my boy back and that's exactly what I did. When the chips are down, you dig deep, you prays hard and you keeps fightin'. There are times in life when you have to put your head down and just work. Nothin' appears to be happening but underneath the earth roots is takin' hold.

When the actor John Travolta was once asked what he did when he experienced barren years and bad reviews between the successful movie Grease *and the movie that relaunched his career* Pulp Fiction, *he replied, "I got up every day and lived. I just kept putting myself out there. I didn't lose faith and I made myself available."*

Exactly. You ain't as dumb as you look. I believe the Good Lord tests us to see if we're ready. He needs to know if we're ready to step up, to stand up and be counted. And if we didn't try to achieve nothin', we wouldn't have no setbacks. Ordinary folk don't take no risks 'cos they're more afraid of losin' than they are of experiencin' the joy of winning. We always have a basic choice.

Was there a turning point in your life for you?

Aside from findin' the Lord, I guess it was findin' I had a voice and I could fight for women's rights. Why, I even met Mr Lincoln at the White House.

I believe you fought for the abolition of segregated street cars?

I did, and I think maybe I sowed a seed for Rosa Parks who did even better than me because she risked her life to stop that practice. Everything is connected. We may not see it in our lifetimes but never underestimate the importance and the value of standing up for what you believe in. Ain't nothing else matters.

What's the biggest lesson you learned?

My experience taught me that if I keeps fightin', I will find a way. If it ain't happenin', I need to ask, "What's the lesson and what's the task I'm being set here? Maybe I need to change direction and do somethin' differently." See, the problem is we all want to blame God for everything. But like I said, God never made me no slave, it was Man. And it wasn't God who punished you. You was punishing your own good self by not havin' the courage to change the things you wanted to change.

That Marianne Williamson was clever when she said, "Our deepest fear is not that we are inadequate. Our deepest fear is that we are powerful beyond measure. It is our light, not our darkness that most frightens us." (Williamson.1996) Nelson Mandela used that in his famous opening address as the new president of South Africa although he didn't credit her. See, people like me made it possible for him to be who he was.

For many our deepest fear is that we're not enough. I know many people are well balanced but it's very rare. We have to learn to harness the experiences that put us there and make them work for us in order to achieve the greatness we all deserve.

In the end it's between you and your Maker. You have to find the answer inside yourself. Look to Him for support, but don't look to Him to do it for you. You gotta meet him halfway.

You suffered terribly and yet you found God. Did you not sometimes think he was a fiction when you were suffering so much?

There you goes again, blaming the Good Lord for Man's inhumanity. It was through my suffering that I found him on the Cross. But my God is the risen God, not the God on the Cross. We all have the answer but we gotta look for it in the right place. There's a story about three Greek gods sitting on a cloud discussing where to hide the Secret of Life. They was worried they'd be exposed as frauds if man found the very simple answer.

The first suggested, "Put it in the outer universe. He'll never reach it."

The second god replied, "That won't work. Man is inquisitive. He'll explore and one day he might find it."

The same god had another suggestion. "Put it under a rock buried in the deepest ocean. Man will never find it there."

"No, that won't work," said the first god. "Man will develop the technology and one day will find it."

Both gods turned to the third god. He was a very old god who'd been sleeping. In unison they asked him, "What do you think, old god?"

"About what?" said the old god, wiping the sleep from his eyes.

"Where shall we hide the Secret to Life so that Man will never find it?" they said impatiently.

"That's simple," replied the old god. "Place it inside man himself. He'll never look there. It's too obvious."

Why don't we do that? The answer is simple. We believe it's gotta be difficult. We gotta find a scroll in a time capsule or listen to a great guru. That's why it always seems out of reach. So, we never expect fulfilment and we don't believe we have the answer. Until we understand what makes us feel the way we do and work through them challenges, we are forever tryin' and failin', failin' and tryin'. We ain't gonna alter our thinking by listenin' to someone givin' us a few rules about limitin' beliefs and a workbook. Sure, we'll feel good for a few weeks or even months but them same ol' messages will start playin' in our heads again.

So what's the answer?

We need to get the beast on the table and deal with it. We have to look the pain in the eye and we have to identify and then deal with the blocks that prevent us from bein' great.

People often ask me what the difference in my life was before I changed my gender role. It's as if there was some great revelation or amazing transformation. But the only thing that changed was my body.

Before, my body was like a car with a manual gearbox, left-hand drive on a British road with flat tyres, no shock absorbers, and no map or GPS satnav. I could go along the road but I was in the wrong vehicle. Everything was a huge effort, everything was painful for me. I was lost and it was agony. I was on a journey but I was going nowhere and the world was overtaking me every day. I was unhappy and everything felt like an act. So was everything wonderful from day one? No, it wasn't. I faced the same challenges, the same problems but at last I was in the right vehicle and I had all the right equipment. Now I could cope with bumpy roads. Driving was easier and gradually it became fun.

There you go then. You'd best get on with it.

Thank you for making it all sound so simple.

14

STANDING UP:
MY COMEDY CAREER

"I get a kick out of being an outsider constantly.
It allows me to be creative."
Bill Hicks

$\longrightarrow\!\!\!\!\!\!\!\infty\!\!\!\!\infty\!\!\!\!\longleftarrow$

When I first began my psychotherapy practice, it was only a part-time occupation. I saw three or four clients each week, my fees were low and they did not financially support me. My course fees, not to mention the hundreds of books I read, meant it cost me to actually practise as a therapist.

I was still saddled with huge debts and so I continued to practise as a financial adviser whilst developing my career as a therapist. I'd never felt financial services was my destiny, but I knew it was the only way I could support my family, which was the primary focus of my life at that time. Marie's income as a schoolteacher made a significant financial contribution towards supporting the girls who were then ten and seven.

Financial services was a great place to be at that time for me because there was a huge amount of support through training and personal development. As well as courses with Tony Robbins I worked with the 'gurus' of the time, people like Brian Tracy, Jay Abrahams, Zig Ziglar, Tom Hopkins and Richard Bandler. I became a Master Practitioner in NLP and did some hypnotherapy training while I continued to study and develop as a Gestalt Psychotherapist.

I worked between twelve and fifteen hours a day, seven days a week. As a financial advisor I decided to specialise in working with small businesses. Although my own business ultimately failed, I understood the psychology and I knew the last car in a company car park at ten o'clock at night was a businessman or woman giving one hundred per cent to try and turn their dream into a reality.

I thought if I helped them to develop their businesses, I would get all their insurance and pension business. Pinning these people down was the big problem. I discussed it with my manager Russ, a flame-haired, red-bearded Irishman.

"You need to join business clubs, breakfast clubs and anywhere you can do a sales presentation," he advised.

I felt gripped by fear. "But I can't do public speaking."

My real fear was that despite countless hours of speech therapy my voice was still very masculine and I felt very self-conscious of my appearance. Of course, I didn't want to share this insecurity with Russ.

"Join a Toastmasters International Club. They'll teach you how to speak in public," was his response.

I discovered there was a Toastmasters International Club thirty minutes' drive away. Not to be confused with the red-jacketed toastmasters at banquets, Toastmasters International is an American organisation which spread around the world to teach people the art of public speaking. The philosophy is the same everywhere. Members work through a series of manuals designed to develop speaking and platform skills. Newcomers reach a basic level of competency when they complete the first manual which includes topics like vocal variety and body language.

They encourage speakers to enter annual competitions. After about a year at Maidenhead Toastmasters they suggested I enter the Humorous Speech competition. To my surprise I won and they entered me into the regional competition. To my further amazement I did well in that too.

The last stage of the competition was the Great Britain and Ireland final which was held in Shannon, Ireland, that year. So, there I was representing the South of England in the final. There were eight finalists all presenting speeches to approximately two hundred people in one of the halls in the ancient castle's grand halls. I was the second to speak and I stepped up to the platform. Once I began, the nerves went and I delivered the speech just about as well as I could.

In time-honoured fashion the results were announced in reverse order, beginning at number four. My name wasn't called out and I held out the hope that I might make the top three. Number three was announced but again it wasn't my name on the judge's lips. Never mind, I thought to myself, making the final was a great achievement for me.

"Second place goes to .... Michelle Bridgman!"

I couldn't believe it. I looked at the other competitors to see if any of them were moving forward. I thought I'd misheard the judge but nobody else moved.

When I finally stepped forward to receive my prize, it felt like an Olympic medal. So, the entrepreneur, the man had failed, but the trans woman with the deep voice, with a voice that got her beaten up when it gave her away, was now standing in front of hundreds of people recognised as the second best speaker in Great Britain.

After I received my award one of the judges approached me and made a remark which was to sow the seed of yet another career that would change my life. She shook my hand warmly.

"That was really funny. You should do stand-up comedy."

Over the following weeks, her words kept coming back to me. As a child I was forever trying to make people laugh. What a crack it would be if the timid trans woman with a deep voice got on stage and performed stand-up. What if I gave it a try, just once?

I trawled through the Internet and Time Out magazine to find a course, or somewhere where I could learn the basics. I found a course at Jacksons Lane Community Centre in Highgate, North London. I'm not sure what I learned on the course other than finding out where a 'newbie' could get 'open spots', a euphemism for getting the chance to perform for free. Reputable promoters and owners of the more established clubs use it as a genuine opportunity to assess new talent. After a couple of spots, if you're good enough you will get a ten minute paid spot, a fifteen minute spot and eventually a twenty minute spot, the normal length for a paid spot on a bill with other comics.

Less reputable promoters try and get acts to come back time and time again on the pretence that they aren't quite good enough. I've seen many give up the comedy circuit because they thought they weren't progressing. Female comedians often have a harder time than their male counterparts. Donna McPhail, a successful comic in the eighties and nineties once told me, "A woman has sixty seconds to prove she is funny, a man has five minutes to prove he isn't."

Some clubs still claim they can't book me on such and such a night because they already have a woman on the bill, yet they wouldn't think twice about having an all male line-up. The assumption is that women aren't funny and the clubs can't risk the night being killed by a bunch of inept women.

One of my comic tutors at Jacksons Lane was a lovely Irish comic called Gina Ryan. She was performing one night in 2000, the last day of my comedy course. Gina was closing the show at a club called Hersterics in Upper Street, Islington, and I went with her to watch. When the girl on the door asked me for my admission fee, Gina interjected with, "It's OK. She's a comic."

So, I was now officially an act! The room was packed when Gina went on to do her twenty minutes. She got laughs and walked off to a good round of applause. I was buzzing. I really wanted to do this.

Gina introduced me to Laura who ran the club and I was given my first five minute open spot six weeks later. Over those six weeks I visited many clubs and watched the performers and I made mental notes of what worked and what didn't. I worked hard to make sure my first date with an audience was successful.

The Thursday finally arrived and I set off for London. I think I probably stopped at every pub or petrol station to use their toilet facilities on my way to Upper Street in Islington, North London. Would they laugh? Would they heckle me and boo me off? Would they realise I'd lived as a man? I arrived and waited for my spot. I was in the middle, the easiest time to work with a warmed up crowd and just before the headliner. On that occasion it was the lovely Catherine Tate, who has since gone on to a very successful career in television. Back then she was already a class act and she was friendly and generous with her feedback to newcomers like me.

The announcer introduced me. "Our next act, please give it up for the wonderful Miss Shelley Cooper!" I chose Cooper because it was my mother's maiden name and, of course, the name of my Granny Cooper. My five minutes went by in a flash and I left the stage to applause, which increased when the compere told the audience it was my first ever gig.

I felt on top of the world. I'd done it. I'd confronted my fear and succeeded. They laughed, they didn't boo and I'd been accepted as female, even if they were curious about my height and my deep voice.

I gave a lift to one of the acts named Teresa who lived en route to my home. She had an infectious enthusiasm and an endearing personality. We have remained friends to this day.

My second gig was at the Comedy Cafe in Rivington Street in the City. The club is run and owned by one of the nicest people in comedy. Noel is a short man, then in his early fifties, with grey spiky hair, who constantly twitched as a result of Tourette's Syndrome. He did a very funny show on the subject at the Edinburgh Festival when he recounted his life story.

The Comedy Cafe was a purpose-built comedy club that seats a couple of hundred people. Driving to the gig I felt nervous but I'd wowed them at Hersterics. What was there to worry about?

But as I entered, I quickly realised this was a different proposition. The room was packed and there was an edge to the atmosphere. A lot of booze was going down and the crowd were up for a raucous night. The host or compere was a man who was building a reputation as an up-and-coming star. Daniel Kitson's always shunned the world of television and media. He just loves performing to a live audience and anyone in comedy will tell you he's right up there with the best.

I don't think there's anyone better than Daniel, Ross Noble or Frankie Boyle when it comes to handling a rowdy comedy room. With his short-sleeved Fairisle sweater and thick milk bottle glasses, Daniel resembled a trainspotter more than a rising comedy star. As soon as he hit the stage he became alive and morphed into a presence that filled the room. Within a minute he had the audience in the palm of his hand. Hecklers were put down with such consummate ease, the audience were barely aware of the challenge. I followed an act from Teesside. It was a guy with material that focused exclusively on body fluids and his ability to masturbate in secret on the London Underground. The audience loved his material and they loved him. I knew my spot would be a long five minutes.

My opening gag worked well at the first gig but it fell flat here. And so did the next, and the next. The audience just gaped at me. I was so bad they didn't even heckle. I swear tumbleweed blew across the stage in a room which was now silent. It's called 'dying on stage'. I can tell you, there is no more apt description of the experience. I walked off to the sound of my own feet, smiling weakly at Noel the club owner as I slipped out into the cold night air. Humiliated, I stepped into my car, slammed the door and burst into tears.

Hundreds of people along with eight other comics had witnessed my demise. Tears rolling down my cheeks, I drove the long slow journey home through the traffic on the City Road, Marylebone Road and A40. I composed myself and resolved that this would not be the way my comedy career would end. Teresa had mentioned a comedy course at the City Lit Institute in London. I would enrol on it and do more gigs until I did one that erased the memory of the Comedy Cafe. I had the rebound factor my father had gifted me, and I knew I'd be back.

There's a popular misconception about comedy. People think the boy or girl making their friends laugh in the pub can simply show up at a comedy club, stand on stage and make people laugh. It may be true for a few gifted individuals and the aim is to make it sound as though the audience are your friends in the pub. There are also people who may be introverted in private but who, like Daniel, come alive on stage. Most fall somewhere in between those two polarities.

At my new comedy class they taught different techniques for writing material and confirmed what I knew already, that you have to share whatever it is that makes you different or what is most obvious about you, whether you're fat, skinny, tall, short, old or young etc. I knew audiences might have doubts over my gender, but I didn't want that to be the focus. Instead I chose to connect with the fact that I knew men found me unattractive. I'd crack really poor gags as I walked on stage like, "I know what you're thinking – Kate Moss." I'd do almost anything rather than own that I'd changed gender.

Jill ran the class and has helped launch the careers of hundreds of comics. At our first class she recommended we avoid doing gigs until we'd learned more techniques. She didn't want anyone to have their confidence destroyed by a bad experience.

A young, neatly dressed man sitting next to me leaned over and whispered, "F*** that, I'm doing Up the Creek tomorrow." That probably sums up Jimmy Carr as a comic; fearless and full of self-belief. Jimmy's rise was spectacular. Within months he was winning competitions and wowing the Edinburgh Festival. I've heard him described as aloof and arrogant but I think it's often because he really is supremely self-confident. In any event he worked really hard for his success.

That hundred per cent self-belief is a must for success in any field and none more so than performing stand-up. Up the Creek was run by the late, legendary Malcolm Hardee and it was notorious for being one of the hardest clubs in the country for aspiring acts, but that didn't bother Jimmy.

Malcolm sometimes paid hecklers so he could judge how resilient new comics were. When I did my first gig there, I got through my set pretty well. As I left the stage, Malcolm returned to the microphone to utter his usual comment for a female act, "Bit rough, but I'd give it one."

After Jill's course I did the rounds of the clubs and I gradually got better. I struggled to get gigs in the bigger clubs and the feedback was always the same … They don't feel comfortable with you. They sense you're holding something back.

I'd dealt with a couple of vicious heckles like "Is it Steve or Shelley?"

"For fifty quid I'll be whoever you want me to be" was my inadequate reply.

It got a laugh but I knew I had to deal with it properly. Avoiding the issue of my gender seemed to be holding me back but I knew I really wanted to continue with stand-up. I had to deal with my block somehow.

Around this time the family and I went for a holiday to the US. My sister-in-law, Gill, had a townhouse in Hudson New York State. We used the house as a base and visited Buffalo, Niagara, the state capital Albany and New York City.

The house was home to hundreds of books sitting on bookshelves in every room. One of them was *Enter Talking* by Joan Rivers. It's a frank account of her childhood and her early career. I believe we don't find books, books find us. The first thing that struck me as I read Joan's book was that she'd been brought up in Catskill, the neighbouring town to Hudson, less than three miles away. Her hilarious accounts of 'gigs from hell', not being paid unless she did well, being told she wasn't good enough, all resonated with me. She wrote, 'Comedy is run by experts who don't know anything.'

I had also been surprised at how unprofessional some of the promoters were. They didn't return calls and I sometimes waited months for my money. Club owners voiced their opinions about acts without knowing anything about them.

Joan talked about trudging around the comedy club circuit without getting any recognition until she suddenly realised she'd improved, yet the clubs remembered her as she was when she started out. It inspired me to get off my backside and work more so I'd get better too. There's a lot of nonsense written about comedy. Being born with comic ability and timing is something of a myth. You have to want to do it badly enough and you must love humour but I believe ninety per cent of it is desire, practise, practise, practise and a dogged determination to succeed. And getting out there every night and just doing it. When he was asked about timing, something for which he was especially noted, the great Jack Benny replied, "It gets better the more I do it."

I returned home from the US with Joan's words ringing in my ears and I resolved to get busy. I also realised I'd have to own my gender identity if I was going to progress. I decided I'd 'come out' at the Edinburgh Festival the following year.

I wrote a show called *Growing Pains* and found a Director in the very talented, irrepressible Lizzie Roper who's a great character actress and comedienne. In 2003 I took my show to Edinburgh and began a three and a half week run. I soon learned that when it comes to critics, you can't win when you're a performer. Reviewers went from telling me I should deal with my change of gender on stage to criticising me for bringing a 'gimmick' as one paper put it, to the festival.

Any performer who's been to the Edinburgh Fringe Festival will tell you there are far too many shows. There aren't too many if you're a member of the public or if you're a club or venue manager. It's the performers who take the risk. If you have a show that doesn't sell tickets, you're likely to lose a shed load of money when you add the cost of accommodation (which, during the festival period, is double the amount normally charged) to the cost of advertising and publicity.

Because there's a plethora of shows to choose from, audiences tend to select which to attend from reviews in newspapers and websites. Anyone can launch a website or a blog and appoint themselves as a critic and acts spend half their time in Edinburgh searching for that elusive four or five star review, which will mean good ticket sales. Any four or five star review is welcome but there are one or two papers that carry extra gravitas.

The Scotsman is such a newspaper and their journalist Kate Copstick is a notoriously tough critic. She's been known to both help launch and destroy the careers of many aspiring comics. A four star review from her is regarded as being the equivalent of a five star from anyone else. On my fourth or fifth night I discovered she was coming to review the show. I wanted a good size audience so I spent all day leafleting because

I couldn't afford to pay anyone else to do it and managed to fill up my sixty-seater room.

That night I got a really positive audience reaction and I was hopeful of a really good review. Later that night I bumped into 'Copstick' as she likes to be known.

"I really enjoyed your show, well done. I think you'll do well."

I was elated. Surely this meant at least a four star review. It was a really good write-up and read like a four star review but despite comments like 'get a ticket, go and see, not to be missed', I got three stars, which basically means good, but not amazing. I was bitterly disappointed.

However, a meeting after this same performance led to a great opportunity. When I came off stage, a young man in his early thirties with a pink Mohican haircut said he had a proposition for me. He looked a bit 'iffy' as they say in East London, so I put him off saying I had to be somewhere and could he call me? How cool was I!

Gary did call the next day and over coffee he explained he owned a production company called Brown Eyed Boy. He had an idea for a sitcom and he wanted to know if I would be interested in being a co-writer and acting in it. "I assume you've done some acting?" he asked. I nodded. Captain Hook in the school play and lessons at the Questors seemed to me to be a qualification. He told me that Stuart, a Controller from the BBC, wanted to come in and see my show to see if he felt I was right for the part they had in mind.

I tried to look cool but I bit his hand off and verbally accepted the provisional offer. Stuart came in and a few weeks later I filmed a pilot in Hampstead, which was used to sell the concept. Early the following year we began developing the characters and writing a full pilot.

Our Director, John Northover, was a taskmaster and very controlling. It was just what I needed since I had absolutely no acting experience, certainly not acting to camera. But when it came to the writing, we lost any control we thought we had. We wrote scenes, went home and rehearsed the lines for the next day, only to return to find it had all changed. This process was debilitating and our original script was unrecognisable. We were all new and, with hindsight, we were not confident enough to challenge the so-called expert writers.

The pilot was duly filmed and in 2004 *Killing Time* was aired on BBC2 and BBC3 along with some other new shows with fresh talent. Our faces were on the cover of the Radio Times and we were all going to be famous and get our own series but in the end the BBC plumped for *The Mighty Boosh* and *Killing Time* was consigned to the dust heap of history. But the whole thing was a great experience and I learned the nuances of scriptwriting and working to camera. It was invaluable and stood me in great stead in the future. I'll always be grateful to Gary for giving me my first break.

I've since completed five one-woman shows in Edinburgh and worked with some wonderful people. As well as Lizzie who directed *Growing Pains*, I worked with directors like Toni Arthur and John Gordillo who has worked with the likes of Eddie Izzard and Michael McIntyre. It always pays to get support by working with talented people and I've been very lucky to collaborate with good professionals.

My most recent show was *Britishness* which played to a full room. I got great reviews so I took the show to Rome and New York. Gabby, the promoter in Rome, filled the room every night for the short run. A Roman entertainment guide ran a piece on me which was produced in both Italian and English. In the centre of the magazine, on one page was a photo and article about me and on the opposite page was a feature on Liza Minnelli. My fantasy was that Liza might read my article. In the holy Eternal City I was transported to heaven.

And if Rome wasn't amazing enough, I took my show to New York for a ten-night run in a theatre just north of Greenwich Village and literally just off Broadway. I love New York as much as I love Rome, so there I was within a couple of weeks performing my one-woman show in my two favourite cities. I booked an apartment in the East Village right next door to the New York chapter of Hells Angels. I figured I wouldn't get mugged or robbed too easily. New York in November is pretty cold but this particular year it was bitter. Unlike Rome, the promoter didn't do so well and I played to small houses.

I've since discovered that unless you have a strong television profile you are a very hard sell in America. This was proved to me one day when the promoter pointed out that a famous 'Briddish' performer (we're not English, Scottish, Welsh or from Northern Ireland in the US) was doing a TV preview in my venue the following night. Russell Brand was in town.

I worked with Russell a few years earlier when I was doing open spots. He was doing a show to try out some material for a TV special he was filming a few days later. I hadn't fully appreciated that Russell, although popular in the UK, was *massive* in America. He sold out within a few minutes of the tickets going on sale. I begged a ticket and went to the show.

After his show, I flyered the exit queue reasoning that if they liked him, they might go for a show called *Britishness*. After the queue had gone I went back into the theatre where Russell was still signing autographs. He caught my eye a couple of times and eventually walked over.

"I'm sure I know you from somewhere but I can't remember where," he said.

"Yeah, it was when I was a shite open spot and you were off your face with heroin several years ago," I replied with a smile on my face.

He laughed. "Oh yes, I remember."

I was a tad disappointed he didn't hit on me. I could have dined out for years on saying no to Russell Brand. But he'd met the gorgeous Katy Perry by then so I was a little outgunned to say the least.

I had a particularly good time at Comic Strip Live which is one of New York's finest. The act before me 'came out' as being a gay man. It was quite obvious that a small section of the audience weren't comfortable with him. That meant they were pretty unlikely to go for either my material or me. But in the end it didn't seem to matter. I 'stormed' it. The audience loved me and they asked me back to do a set the next night.

I've learned a lot from doing comedy. There is no better grounding for any performance skills than standing in a room full of strangers, trying to make them laugh. When it goes well, there's nothing like it for a great buzz. Performing comedy has given me overall confidence as a person. It taught me that if I could handle a group of people who were not politically correct or polite and still connect with them, what on earth did I have to worry about in wider society?

Comedy works best if you can be self-deprecating without putting yourself down. Audiences need permission to laugh with you. They don't feel comfortable about laughing *at* you. That's why they can be vicious with acts who are dying. They can't stand the pain either and want to end it quickly. I'm now upfront with my change of gender on stage but I quickly move on to topics that engage me. The rule of stand-up is that you have to have an attitude towards your material. Love it or hate it but you *can't* be indifferent towards it.

IMAGINARY CONVERSATION WITH JOAN RIVERS

"I succeeded by saying what everyone else is thinking."
Joan Rivers

Joan Rivers is a comedy inspiration *and* a human inspiration. She has overcome personal setback after professional setback after personal setback throughout her life. She's probably the most persistent and determined of my heroes and sheroes. On stage she is a tour de force. No subject is beyond the reach of her waspish tongue and she's impervious to the sensitivities of her audience. In a man's world she reigned as Queen of Comedy for more than three decades. I wanted to ask her what qualities she drew on to keep faith and keep going, even when everything looked bleak. Reading her book *Enter Talking* was an inspiration when I needed it.

How did you keep going in those early days when it seemed like you weren't progressing?

There's an old saying that goes, "She who earns no money ain't going to eat tonight," or in my case, "If you're crap, you gotta get better at what you're doing."

Typical Joan. Down to basics. Is that the real Joan Rivers?

Honey, nothing about me is real. I've had more plastic surgery than a Madame Tussauds waxwork dummy. The whole world knows that. Listen, I may be famous but fame doesn't pay the rent. I'm like every other performer. I'm as good as my last performance. Period.

Is that attitude a throwback to when you were a struggling performer?

Maybe. I spent so long dragging myself round New York doing open spots they never paid me for. I know how fragile this fame thing is. One minute everyone loves you and the next you're a leper.

Do you really feel like that?

Get you, Miss I-don't-care-what-anyone-thinks-of-me Shelley!

Touché. I suppose it's because I look up to you as one of my heroes and I imagine you to be immune from this stuff.

I do what you did. I put on a front although frankly I don't give a f*** anymore. What's all this hero shit anyway? We all do this stuff because we're driven to do it. Don't tell me you never died on your arse out there.

Of course I did. What's the secret technique for letting go of worrying about what people think of you?

In the beginning I did worry. I was always struggling to make it happen. The secret? Ha! If there is one, please tell me. I guess I think the secret is to give the audience everything but not be invested in the reaction. If they get you, they get you. Here's the problem, Shelley. If you're invested in their response and you look for laughs, it becomes false. It's like love. You only get true love back when you give true love without demanding it back. It's a kinda universal law.

That's why I'm so thrilled to be talking to you. It's that courage I admire so much.

You do what you gotta do, honey.

I've always loved your work and then I had this spooky experience I talk about in my book.

Oh please! You didn't fantasise about me, did you?

It wasn't that kind of spooky. No, I was staying in a town called Hudson.

Now that's what I call spooky. Hudson is a 'shit hole'. I mean, please!

Your book found me. Your biography Enter Talking *was on the bookshelf and I read it. Then I realised your town, Catskill, where you grew up, is the next town along. When I read about you out and about in New York City, with your tape recorder being rejected night after night but never giving up, I was so inspired.*

What the hell made you want to read that? You were on holiday for Heaven's sake. You ever been in therapy? God, you must need it.

Something you said really stuck with me when you said, "Comedy is run by experts who know nothing."

It's true and you know why? It's because most promoters and critics haven't got the balls. No offence to you, honey! But we sure have.

But what drove you to keep on going?

I don't really know. I guess I just really wanted to do it. You get that, don't you?

Absolutely, I do.

It's that drive that says get out there and knock 'em dead.

Is it easier now?

Hell no, it's just different. You know what I think? In some ways it gets harder. When you're new on the scene, you expect to die and no one knows who the hell you are anyway. Now, they expect me to kill, every time. If I'm not very funny, the whole frigging world knows about it.

Have you offended many people?

Oh, please! I can't believe you even asked me that. Of course I have. My whole act's based upon shocking people and pissing them off.

Why do you do that?

Because I hate the sanitised shit we get on television. I say what people are really thinking. That's why I did gags about the Twin Towers. It pissed people off but I can't tell you the number of people who loved it. Comedy is not just about laughter, it's about making people think, making them question their values.

That's what I love about you. You go where other comics won't. I think I'd like to do more of that.

Well, get out there and do it, Shelley! You'll piss some people off, sure, but others'll love you for it and d'you know why? They'll love you because you're brave enough to say what you think and you'll be speaking for them. Comedy works best when we reflect back what society's too scared to say.

You've often been quoted as saying that you joked about your husband's suicide because it was the only way you got through it. What did you mean?

The pain was so intense, I coped by cracking gags. For those brief moments the laughter overcame the pain because I could deny it before it came flooding back. That's why a lot of people connected with the Twin Towers gags.

Was there something about people hearing your pain?

I think there was. Being on stage is where you and I get our connection. It isn't real on one level but then it *is* very real on another, but that makes it all the more compelling. We go off into our fantasy world for a few minutes and then shock people into engaging with us.

I've always wanted to know how you pulled off that stunt to get on the Carson Show when you were shunned by all the other TV networks. What happened?

Nobody would give me a break so my agent booked me in another name. By the time they realised they'd been had, it was too late to book someone else. Johnny Carson said those immortal words, "You're going to be a star," and the rest is history.

That took some guts, Joan.

Well it did, but I was desperate to succeed. When you want something badly enough and you take action, it happens. I just would not be denied.

Any advice for a performer?

Take risks and do it the way you want to, even if everyone tells you not to.

If you could sum up your success in a sentence, what would you say?

I'd say who the f*** are you to tell me to only use one sentence! No really, I'd say take risks. Don't get to the end of your life without knowing you gave everything you got.

Because your life could end tomorrow?

Jeez, you're quick!! That's the whole point. You gotta get out there and do it now.

15

COMING HOME:
CONVERSATION WITH ME

"I was arrested by an inquiry, the purport of which did not reach me, but which seemed to be addressed by myself, and was preferred in a soft sweet voice that struck me very pleasantly. I turned hastily round and found at my elbow a pretty little girl, who begged to be directed to a certain street at a considerable distance, and indeed in quite another quarter of the town.

'It is a very long way from here,' said I, 'my child.'

'I know that, sir,' she replied timidly. 'I am afraid it is a very long way, for I came from there tonight.'

'Alone?' said I in some surprise.

'Oh yes, I don't mind that, but I am a little frightened now, for I have lost my road.'

'And what made you ask it of me? Suppose I should tell you wrong.'

'I am sure you will not do that,' said the little creature. 'You are such a very old gentleman, and walk so slowly yourself.'"

Charles Dickens, *The Old Curiosity Shop*

———◦○◦———

It took a long time for me to find a spiritual path. Kicking and scream-ing, I came to the realisation that the man from Nazareth, a humble carpenter named Jesus, had given a perfect template for living our lives. Jesus is my last hero and the only one I speak with daily in my pleadings and reflections. Much as I admire my other heroes and sheroes, he is the only one I would bow down to. I can only share that when I was in the abyss, my voice was heard and I was lifted up. Faith is what it says it is. Just that. Faith. It is a belief that comes from the deepest knowing of our souls; not something that can be proved with science or any amount of historical research.

Sadly the church mostly gets the message distorted and spends too much of its time judging or excluding people, including me when I changed gender, rather than sharing the message of love and forgiveness and leaving God to do the judging. It's called Grace. Sadly, too many Christians in Christian churches are anything but Christian.

It would be easy to say my life is about change but changing ourselves is a myth. As Beisser tells us, we can only change to become who we *are*. My life, like all lives, is a journey and a quest for knowledge and understanding. I seem to have spent my life searching for myself more than anything else and I've probably been too intense at times. My English teacher, Mr Wingate, once told me, "Don't forget to stop and smell the roses." He clearly saw a side of me I wasn't aware of. But so often we don't see ourselves as clearly as our observers.

When we seek heroes, sheroes, mentors or guides we need to be clear that they cannot live our lives for us and nor should they. At some point we have to learn that we *are* enough. We have to trust ourselves and accept our own decisions without remorse or regret. We have to become our *own* hero or shero. My journey has made me realise that actually my real hero, Jesus apart, is me, just as it should be for everyone.

For my last reflection and conversation with my last shero I'm going to hold up a mirror and speak to the part of myself I don't trust enough — my intuition. When I look at myself in the mirror, I see someone who's come a long way, someone whose struggles took them to the brink of oblivion, someone who made it back step by step to a happy and productive life. From my earliest memory of feeling different, I asked myself the same questions over and over. And now I'm going to ask myself once again. This time I know I have some of the answers, and more than ever before I'm at last at peace with myself.

There are times in life when you have to put your head down and just work. Like Sojourner Truth says, "It may appear nothing's happening but you just have to trust that beneath the earth, roots are taking place." I believe our Maker tests us to see if we're ready. Frightened people don't take risks because they're more afraid of losing than they are of experiencing the joy of winning. We have a basic choice. Experience has taught me that if I keep fighting, I will find a way.

If it's not happening, I need to ask, "What's the lesson here?" You may be thinking, *Well it's ok for you, you're a therapist and you've had time to study this.* And you're right. It *is* ok for me. But the real question is, 'Is it ok for you?' If it's not, are you prepared to take the time and put in the effort? You have to find the answer inside yourself. So why don't you? Many of us never believe we're enough for the world. Either that, or we think we're *too* much for it. By the way, this is an important distinction as we either spend our lives fearing rejection or fearing we aren't good enough. We don't expect fulfilment, we think we don't deserve it and we certainly don't believe we can find the answers. Until we understand the factors that cause us to feel the way we do and have worked through them, we are always trying and failing, trying and failing. We need to face ourselves and deal with it.

People often ask me, "What was the biggest difference in your life after you changed gender role?" It's as if they think there was some great revelation or amazing transformation. But the only thing that changed was my body and my peace of mind. So was everything wonderful from day one when I changed gender? No, it wasn't. I faced the same challenges, the same problems but at least now I was in the right vehicle and I had all the right equipment. I could cope with bumpy roads, driving was easier and gradually, bit by bit, life became fun.

Too many people struggling with gender identity come into my psychotherapy practice holding the mistaken belief that life will become amazing as soon as they step off the operating table. But the world is still the same and if, and only *if*, it's the right decision for them will it eventually give them the possibility for their lives to be better. But we can never escape from who we truly are.

Why did this happen to me? What am I supposed to learn from this experience?

I now realise that taking on the role of victim was very arrogant of me. Was I really any different, any more special? Everyone has their own unique experience and their own personal challenges. My challenges were just more unusual. And unlike millions of people, I didn't have to overcome physical disability or an abusive upbringing. I wasn't born in the Third World, where survival itself is a daily pursuit. All experience is relative.

I believe we all have a mission. For some it results in material wealth and high profile success; for others it may be a quieter, less conspicuous mission which nevertheless has an impact on the world.

What have I learned about my life's purpose?

All of us have a responsibility to work on our missions but my early searching came from a very egotistical place. Surely my purpose was to invent a light bulb or find a cure for cancer? Perhaps it is simply to serve God by serving mankind with whatever gifts we have.

I learned that my life's purpose would have no meaning if it had been clear from the beginning. What need would there be for searching? What need would be there for learning? Life's purpose isn't an event. It's a process. Without my struggles nothing would have provided the rich opportunity for growth that I was given. My purpose continues to unfold and evolve in an ever-changing system of events. My crime would be to ignore the gifts bestowed upon me.

So are our attitudes and beliefs shaped by the great unseen or is it all learned?

We're all born without neurosis. When we are born, it is without the life experiences and parenting which later shapes us. But I wonder if that's strictly true? Our existence doesn't begin when we're born into the world. It is when we are conceived that we begin our journey and that journey begins in the womb. Birth is just a stage, an announcement that we can let go of the placenta and rely on our own lungs and organs to begin life outside. We know to some degree we inherit our personalities from our parents but our subconscious also begins to develop while we're still in the womb. Studies have shown we can pick up energies and emotions before we are born. A fearful or grieving mother may transmit those emotions to their unborn child. I believe my mother transmitted the pain of the loss of her first-born to me through the placenta, just as at the same time she was nourishing me. I was born with that sadness within me.

And it goes deeper. Bert Hellinger, a leader in the field of Family Systems Therapy, and practitioners who work in this field, tell us our thoughts and desires are influenced by our ancestors and that the generations of our families are interconnected. After all, is personality a chance piece of genetic engineering or is it a handing on from those that came before us?

In the West, especially when we seek to find out why we're here, we obsess about our purpose in life as though it's a single event or experience. But we're constantly shifting and the world we live in is always changing.

Zen Buddhists quote the story of the student who asked Buddha, "Can a man step into the same river twice?"

"No," came the reply, "for he is not the same man and it is not the same river."

So, we just have to meet our challenges as best we can without fearing failure or even as we sometimes do, success.

Rudyard Kipling wrote, 'If you can meet with Triumph and Disaster and treat those two impostors just the same.'

So can experience alone grant us wisdom?

Experience is just that, nothing more and nothing less, just experience. It's what we learn from it and what we do with it that matters. When we are young, we imitate our parents and siblings. At some point we have to separate and make our own decisions. If we are not empowered to experience independence early enough, we may experience the narcissistic wound I talked about earlier and our mantra is 'I am not enough'. Conversely, if we are or feel abandoned by our 'loved' ones we experience ourselves as being 'too much' for the world.

My parents loved me and although my father was distant, I knew he was the great provider for our family. They did their best but I was not allowed to separate and grow early enough. My mother feared the death of a second child too much and she was overprotective. That came from love so I can't blame her. And that wound is at the root of so many limiting beliefs in my life.

My feeling that I'd only have a valid existence if I helped others made me want to work as a psychotherapist. By healing my clients I thought I'd reaffirm my value to myself and my pain of fearing I wasn't enough would be diminished. I'd be healed. It didn't work. I only began to heal when I accepted myself, not when others accepted me.

So who makes a good teacher?

We don't learn about ourselves by being told something. We learn from coming to our own understanding through our own experience and when we feel free to experiment, seek knowledge and explore without fear of failure or reprimand. We cannot really teach people anything. The best teachers facilitate a process where they guide and lead their pupils to their own understanding.

So how do we create fulfilling connections and relationships?

Connection happens when we're available and willing to try and step into the other's experience to understand them. It's not the understanding but the act of *seeking* to understand and asking the right questions. The fact that we're willing to try is, in itself, healing.

In the end I think real connection comes when we realise we have to be grounded in our own separateness. Only then are we in a position to honour the difference in the people we meet. Only then can we can experience genuine connectedness.

Why did I avoid connecting with myself for so long?

My love of travel was born of a restless spirit. It became a perfect vehicle for me to keep moving and avoid being with myself. We are all very creative in finding ways to avoid pain. Sadly it can take a long time before we realise that the pain is only present in the avoidance. When I faced up to my own truth, I learned to be at peace.

Do we all need to struggle with our identity before finding who we are?

I don't think we all need to struggle but if we never question or challenge ourselves, we never find out who we really are. In my case it wasn't a matter of choice. I had a mind and body that seemed intent on divorce. However foolish it now seems, I chose to struggle against it and to fight myself. Had I not been so afraid of rejection and what the world might think of me, I would have come to terms with my predicament earlier. In fact it wouldn't have been a predicament at all. It would have been a simple matter of self-acceptance and in so doing giving myself permission to live fully in the moment. At some point the bargaining with God has to stop and we have to just *be*. The alternative is to constantly create our own struggle.

But how do we cope with despair?

George Eliot wrote in her book *Middlemarch*, 'But what we call our despair is often only the painful eagerness of unfed hope.' I think frustration and despair only take root when we dare ourselves to hope. If we were content to live sheltered lives and to hide our gifts from the world, we wouldn't know frustration or despair but we would feel dead. To live we have to take risks. To feel alive we sometimes have to live on the edge. That is why men and women climb mountains, sail around the world and travel at great speed. It is in those moments when we're close to the edge that we feel truly alive. If I hadn't come close to failing and even to death itself, I wouldn't know the true joy of living.

How do we cope with fear of rejection?

One of the prerequisites for a stage performer and especially comics is to not be invested in the audience liking you. I'm not saying a performer shouldn't care about their audience. Indeed they must, for indifference towards an audience would result in certain death on stage. But if I worried about every audience liking everything about me, it would result in safe, middle-of-the-road material that would neither entertain them nor satisfy me, the performer. Just look at some of the comedy on our television screens.

This risk-taking is one of the reasons people are fascinated by comedy and comedians. If I had applied this philosophy in my everyday life,

I'd have profited greatly from it a lot earlier. But for far too long I was stifled by fear. Fear of rejection, fear of failure and fear of not feeling fulfilled. I grew up in a family where death, loss and lack had hit my parents hard. My mother's fear of loss when I was both inside and outside her womb must have a place in forming me and my personality with all its glorious failings and strengths.

I think I grew up fearing everything. On a beach she'd tell me, "Don't go out too far," before I'd even arrived at the water. And "Don't go too near the edge," when I stood on a station platform, as if the extraordinary loud noise of a steam engine wasn't a big enough deterrent!

So are we destined to carry our neuroses around with us for the rest of our lives?

Absolutely and unequivocally NO! Not if we find out the reasons for our behavioural patterns and then change them. That is the one thing we can change about ourselves.

So what's the antidote to fear?

The antidote is faith. At an existential level all fear is fear of death itself but even in our daily lives we will meet fear. When we accept there is no failure, or perhaps that the only failure is not to fully take part in the game of life. When we do, the fear recedes. We have to *just do it*. We have to allow ourselves to feel fear but say, *"I will take action,"* in spite of that fear. That is why being a leader is not about getting people to follow. Great leaders take action and inspire others to follow.

Ultimately, we can only fear ourselves. When we have faith and we know ourselves then we know we have nothing on earth to be afraid of.

When we begin to love ourselves and find something more important than ourselves to love and even something worth dying for, we begin to live a fulfilled life and become the light in the world we were meant to be.

EPILOGUE

Standing at my sister's grave I feel the warmth of family connection, the sadness of loss and the certainty of life's longing for itself. All life at its end seems very short. My sister lived for only four months and yet the impact of her life continues. Just like the ripple in a pond, our lives impact on others long after we've gone.

My sister's lonely grave in what is now Israel seems very close to home.

ACKNOWLEDGEMENTS

This book had its roots long before I was born.

To the grandfather who rescued his horse on the fields of Flanders in the Great War and to those before him I have never met … yet passed me the baton of life.

I thank the sister I never knew but whose death made space for me on the earth. To my parents who always loved me, fed and clothed me through great hardship. To my sister Geraldine for being my childhood protector and my close friend. To my sister Penny who found me too difficult to cope with yet provided a balance that I've needed.

I owe thanks to my psychotherapist, Judith, who by her example taught me more about being a therapist than anyone before or since. My tutors and my psychotherapy supervisor, Maria, who possesses more wisdom and insight into the human condition than anyone I have ever met. I have many friends through psychotherapy, most notably Joan and her lovely husband Vic, Irene, Colin, Isabelle and Winnie. To Julie Gunn and Jane Noble Knight who read and shared thoughts on the manuscript as it grew. To Lynn Serafinn who encouraged me to write the book and whose book *The Garden of the Soul* sowed the seed which grew into the format.

To my dear friend, Valerie, without whose love and support I would not be here. To Teresa who is quite simply the funniest and loveliest person on earth. To my dear friend, the very talented Jason Wood, who lost his life at the early age of 38 and to Helen who also left us far too early. To Paula for always being there and offering encouragement.

I have been blessed with many friends and will inevitably miss someone but I will nevertheless try. My longest friendship … Dave, my Aussie man's man, Aitor, Emma, Gwynne, Jane, Brenda, Jan and Tony and even the friends I lost when my life changed too dramatically for them to cope with.

No mention of my life would be complete without including my family who have quite simply been the most amazing gift any human being could possibly have. My daughters, Laura and Susie, who have gifted unconditional love beyond measure and my beautiful granddaughter, Kerra, who has given me renewed inspiration and joy.

ABOUT THE AUTHOR

Michelle (Shelley) Bridgman is an author, scriptwriter, stand-up comic, actor, professional speaker and psychotherapist. Regularly appearing on television and radio news programmes as well as in print media, she has been described as one of the world's leading authorities on gender identity.

She describes her interest in psychotherapy as having its roots in what she thought of as her own 'madness' before coming to terms with her need to change her gender in the 1980s. Shelley worked as a Samaritan volunteer for seventeen years and began studying Counselling in 1989. Having left school at fifteen with no qualifications, she attained a Masters degree in Psychotherapy at the age of 57 and is currently completing a Doctoral research project.

As a means of overcoming her fear of speaking in public she joined a Toastmasters International speaking club and was runner up in the Great Britain humorous speech contest in 1997. A chance comment by a judge who said, "You should do stand-up," inspired a career change. As 'Shelley Bridgman' she now performs on the UK's comedy circuit and has performed five one woman shows at The Edinburgh Festival. Shelley took her show *Britishness* to Edinburgh, Rome, New York and the Leicester Square Theatre in London.

In 2005 Shelley co-wrote and starred in a sitcom which was aired on BBC television. In 2012 she won the Silver Stand-up competition and was voted the UK's best comic over the age of 55. She has visited over sixty countries and is a regular keynote speaker at conferences inspiring audiences to own their strengths by being who they were born to be.

Shelley has been married for forty years, has two grown up daughters and a granddaughter.

You can find out more about Shelley's work at www.stand-upforyourself.com or www.facebook.com/standupforyour or by sending an email to shelley@stand-upforyourself.com.

REFERENCES

Beisser Arnold (1970) *The Paradoxical Theory of Change,* Fagan J & Shepherd I (Eds) Gestalt Therapy Now. Harper & Row, New York

Camus, Albert, (1947) *The Plague.* Translated by Stuart Gilbert

Eliot, George (1983) *Middlemarch.* Wordsworth Classics

Emerson, Ralph Waldo,(2012) *The Essential Writings of Ralph Waldo Emerson.* Renaissance Classics

Frankl, Viktor (1984) *Man's Search for Meaning.* Ebury Press

Gibran, Kahlil (1973) *The Prophet,* Alfred A Knopf - hardback edition

Kipling, Rudyard (2011) *If,* from *Collected Poems.* Phoenix Press

Lee, Laurie (1968) *As I Walked Out One Midsummer Morning.* Penguin Books

Marx, Groucho (1978) *The Groucho Letters.* Sphere Books

Marx, Groucho (1975) *Memoirs of a Mangy Lover.* Futura Books

Milligan, Spike (1963) *Puckoon.* Penguin Books

Oriah Mountain Dreamer (1999) *The Invitation.* Harper Collins

Rivers, Joan, with Merryman, Richard (1987) *Enter Talking.* Star Publishing

Stevenson, Robert Louis (2004) *Travels with a Donkey in the Cevennes.* Penguin Classics

Truth, Sojourner – McKissack, Patricia and Frederick (1992) *Ain't I a Woman?* Scholastic Inc

Williamson, Marianne (1996) *A Return to Love.* Harper Paperbacks, New York